TWAYNE'S WORLD AUTHORS SERIES
A Survey of the World's Literature

SPAIN

Janet W. Díaz, Texas Tech University

Gerald Wade, Vanderbilt University

EDITORS

Eighteenth–Century Spanish Literature

TWAS 526

Francisco de Paula José
Goya y Lucientes

"Scene of Witchcraft" — 1798

EIGHTEENTH-CENTURY
SPANISH LITERATURE

By R. MERRITT COX

TWAYNE PUBLISHERS
A DIVISION OF G. K. HALL & CO. BOSTON

Published in 1979 by Twayne Publishers,
A division of G. K. Hall & Co.
All Rights Reserved

Printed on permanent/durable acid-free paper and bound
in the United States of America

First Printing

Library of Congress Cataloging in Publication Data

Cox, Ralph Merritt, 1939–
Eighteenth-century Spanish literature.

(Twayne's world authors series; TWAS 526: Spain)
Bibliography: p. 151–57
Includes index.
1.   Spanish literature—18th century—History and criticism.
I.   Title
PQ6069.C65   860'.9'004   78–14846
ISBN 0-8057-6367-8

For Dick Austin

Contents

About the Author

R. Merritt Cox was born in Richmond, Virginia, in 1939 and holds advanced degrees from the University of Wisconsin. He has taught at that university, at Duke University, and is now Professor of Spanish at the College of William and Mary. He belongs to the honorary societies Phi Beta Kappa, Sigma Delta Pi, and Phi Alpha Theta. In December, 1971, he was elected a Corresponding Member of The Hispanic Society of America. He has received various scholarships and fellowships that have enabled him to study both here and abroad. He has published widely, particularly in materials relating to the Spanish eighteenth century. His books include biographies of the Englishman John Bowle — the first editor of *Don Quixote,* Tomás de Iriarte, and Juan Meléndez Valdés. His papers and articles cover a spectrum of subjects from Fray Martín Sarmiento to Spanish relations with the English colonies and the United States in the 1700s. He brings many of these varied interests together here in his analysis of Spain and her literature in the eighteenth century.

Preface

The literature of Spain during the 1700s has only recently received much serious consideration. Heretofore it has often been cursorily surveyed, sometimes dismissed as relatively unimportant, and not often appreciated except by a few scholars. Happily we are witnessing today a much more fair and sympathetic interest in the period itself and in its literary productions.

Divided into four chapters discussing literary, cultural, and social directions, the present work provides a general look at the writers and their works. Because of the enormous amount of material covered and the resultant need for selectivity, I may have excluded or given little notice to an author that the reader feels deserved attention. For example, he may wonder at the relatively few pages on Cadalso and Torres Villarroel. The reason is that Cadalso and Torres both are excellently analyzed in more detailed studies than this one. At the same time, it is also hoped that any stress on previously ignored works of a writer or on a literary figure himself will lead the reader to see the untapped wealth in the literature of this period.

For the quotations in the text I have chosen not to present the Spanish but only the English translations. These latter are my own except for those from Iriarte's *Literary Fables*. The reason for not including the Spanish is, again, the space involved.

A few words about the bibliography are in order here. It is as general and ample as I thought it could be made for a study of this length. For the most part, I have listed easily accessible works and those that, taken as a group, present a variety of viewpoints.

R. MERRITT COX

College of William and Mary

Chronology

1700   Death of Charles II, who is succeeded by Philip V, thus bringing the Bourbons to the Spanish throne.

1701   Beginning of the War of the Spanish Succession.

1702   Ignacio de Luzán is born (d. 1754).

1703   Birth of José Francisco de Isla (d. 1781).

1712   National Library is founded.

1713   Treaty of Utrecht is signed, ending the War of the Spanish Succession, and the Royal Academy of the Language is founded.

1724   Philip V abdicates in favor of his son Luis, who dies in the same year, causing his father to become king once more.

1726   Benito Jerónimo Feijoo publishes the first volume of his *Teatro crítico universal* (*Universal Theater of Criticism*). The Royal Academy of the Language begins publishing its *Diccionario de autoridades*. Both publications continue until 1739.

1731   Birth of Ramón de la Cruz (d. 1794).

1734   Birth of Vicente García de la Huerta (d. 1787).

1737   *Diario de los literatos de España* (*Diary of the Writers of Spain*) and Luzán's *Poética* (*Poetics*). Nicolás Fernández de Moratín is born (d. 1790).

1739   The Royal Academy of History is founded.

1741   Birth of José Cadalso (d. 1782).

1742   *Sátira contra los malos escritores de este siglo* (*Satire Against the Bad Writers of This Century*). Feijoo begins publication of his *Cartas eruditas y curiosas* (*Intellectual Letters*).

1744   Gaspar Melchor de Jovellanos is born (d. 1811).

1746   Philip V dies and is succeeded by Ferdinand VI.

1750   Birth of Tomás de Iriarte (d. 1791).

1752   The Academy of Fine Arts of Saint Ferdinand is founded.

1754   Birth of Juan Meléndez Valdés (d. 1817).

1759   Ferdinand VI dies and is succeeded by Charles III.

1760   Birth of Leandro Fernández de Moratín (d. 1828).

1761   Family Compact is first signed aligning France and Spain militarily.
1764   Feijoo dies (b. 1676).
1766   Esquilache riots.
1767   Expulsion of the Jesuits.
1770   Death of Diego de Torres Villarroel (b. 1694).
1779   Tomás Antonio Sánchez publishes the *Poema de mío Cid.*
1781   John Bowle's edition of *Don Quixote.*
1782   Iriarte's *Fábulas literarias* (*Literary Fables*).
1788   Charles III dies and is succeeded by Charles IV.
1789   The French Revolution begins.

CHAPTER 1

Spanish Society in the 1700s

I *The Bourbon Kings*

T HE eighteenth century in Spain has long been an enigma to many people. It is not so much a mystery in itself, however. The main problem has been the failure of scholars and students in general to realize exactly what is there. This tendency to see incorrectly has been especially evident in respect to the period's literature. Most critics, until the last fifteen years, lightly passed over it or discussed only certain aspects that interested them. Often their insight was keen and new ideas did come forth. More often than not their views were biased and followed the usually antagonistic tones of Menéndez y Pelayo, who, rightly or wrongly, is the critic most responsible for the generally antagonistic attitude toward the 1700s. Since about 1960 we have witnessed a new interest among critics about eighteenth-century Spanish literature. New, more intellectually respectable attitudes have come to be accepted, but still not without some opposition. To a degree, it is as if the feuding and constant polemics that were so much a part of the cultural and social scene two hundred years ago have continued among the critics who today write about it.

From the very first page of our study, then, we must realize that we shall be examining a century of inordinate intellectual conflict. We must realize too that our ideas about that time are still being formed through conflicting interpretations. If we approach the people, their history, and their cultural output with a degree of innocent searching we can nevertheless obtain an accurate view of their lives and their most outstanding achievements.

This century of controversy in all spheres began precisely in controversy — the War of the Spanish Succession. The Hapsburg dynasty that had ruled Spain since 1517 came to an inglorious end in 1700 with the death of Charles II. The seventeenth century had been one of continuous political decline that was rather accurately reflected in its three monarchs. Charles II was a child physically on ascending the throne in 1665 and remained so mentally for the rest of his life. The French, whose power had been increasing since the early 1600s under the leadership of Richelieu, were the stronger European power by the late 1600s. Within a hundred years there had occurred a complete reversal of the Spanish-French political relationship, insofar as military power and influence in Europe were concerned.

Looking for a moment at the reign of Charles II, we can see the distressing state of the nation in 1700. The king, infirm physically and mentally, was incapable of producing an heir. He was not expected to reach the age that he did. With the constant expectation of his death there was much plotting for control of the throne once he should die. Behind all the machinations was Louis XIV, who was determined to have the Spanish throne for his grandson Philip of Anjou. The poor Spanish king was beset in his own family by the queen-mother, María Ana, who preferred her own House of Austria. Louis XIV, to keep the political situation all the more intolerable, declared a series of wars on Spain in which he was joined by a succession of allies, who were interested in what they could get from Spain. The various wars occurred in 1667–1668, 1672–1678, 1681–1684, and 1689–1697.

England, recovering at last from her own rather unsettled seventeenth century, desired the elevation of the Archduke Charles of Austria to the Spanish throne. He was the son of the Holy Roman Emperor. England naturally did not want to see the French Bourbons extend their control over Spain. The Spanish king, increasingly incapable, was gradually forced into a major domestic and political quandary. The Austrian faction bombarded him through his new Austrian wife and through the king's confessor. The French group succeeded in persuading Charles that his wife was seeking to have him killed. In a fit of desolation he changed confessors, the new one being of the French faction. In 1700 the king took to what would be his death bed. This still did not halt the plotting. On October 3 he named Philip as sole heir to all his dominions and on November 1 he died.

If it had not been for Louis XIV's arrogance, the War of the Spanish Succession, as it came to be called, might have been avoided. Initially after Charles II's death most of the quarreling factions seemed placated by the choice of Philip V as the new Spanish king. The only group completely opposed to him was that of the Hapsburg archduke. As long as there seemed to be no real possibility that France and Spain would be ruled by one monarch, England and other potential enemies did not disapprove of the resolved situation. However, Louis, feeling quite confident in his supposed role of European arbiter, recognized in Philip the rights of succession to the French throne and had the proper documents recorded before the Parliament of Paris. This politically blundering move and some other unfortunate actions created a situation totally unacceptable to the other contestants. England and the Protestant Netherlands joined with Austria and the Holy Roman Empire in 1701 in an alliance for open war against Spain and France. The Hapsburgs of course were desirous of continuing their family rule in Spain. England especially was thinking of her commercial interests, since she feared the end of her expansion in the New World by the joining of Spanish and French power. This fear dominated all the wars between the English and Spanish in the rest of the century.

The war itself actively began in 1702 and Spain was one of the main fields of combat. In fact, the Peninsula experienced a kind of civil war, since the Catalans, as well as the Portuguese, sided with the English. Thus Spain began the internecine conflict that still plagues her today. The anti-Bourbons were never as successful as they had expected to be. With the exception of the seizure of Gibraltar in 1704 their achievements were not large. This fact, plus the ascension of the archduke to the throne of the Holy Roman Empire in 1711 as Charles VI, caused Spain's enemies to desist somewhat in their activity. The prospect of an Austro-Spanish empire was no more pleasing to England than a Franco-Spanish one. Between 1711 and 1714 several treaties were signed. The most important was that of Utrecht in 1713; for all practical purposes this treaty ended the War of the Spanish Succession. The most important results for both England and Spain were Philip's renunciation for himself and his heirs of any rights to the throne of France and the cession of Gibraltar to England.[1] In most respects the treaty was favorable to Spain. Her failure to realize this fully caused her further political conflicts with England in the years to come.

This war, then, set the stage for much of Spain's political activity in the eighteenth century. The need she felt to combat English encroachment explains her involvement in all the conflicts, especially the American Revolution. More damaging actually was the, at times, uncomfortable new relationship with France. While on many occasions political acumen and, very significantly, the Spanish populace itself would dictate an estrangement from French-induced foreign involvements, the Spanish government would pursue goals that all too frequently caused the nation grief. This war that began the century definitively ended nearly two hundred years of one familial leadership and established another that curiously was as ambivalent about its relations to the people as they themselves were sometimes about their proper recognition of it. The Bourbons in general sought to retrieve Spain from its state of decadence. In this they reflect the attempts of all the *Ilustrados* with whom we shall become acquainted in the following pages. Just like some of those enlightened men, however, they sometimes were not exactly certain of which road to follow. This century was to be one of driving energy, of tremendous desires, and great ideals. It would also witness much bungling and hesitation and endless backbiting.

To enumerate the changes of alliance between Spain, England, France, and Austria in the first half of the century would be almost endless. Two aims were uppermost in the policy of the Spanish government during this period: a futile desire on Philip's part to be king of France should Louis XV die and the perseverance of Philip's second wife, Isabel Farnesio of Parma, in her desire to secure Italian thrones for her children. Philip's short-lived abdication in 1724 in favor of his eldest son Luis I may be partially explained by his wish to seem politically inactive when Louis XV should die. This much-longed-for death always eluded Philip. Luis died of tuberculosis in the same year he ascended the throne and Philip once more became king.

Isabel Farnesio is certainly one of the most fascinating characters of the century. Philip had earlier been married to María Luisa of Savoy, who died quite young, greatly loved by the Spanish people. Isabel married Philip in 1714, the same year that his first wife died. From the beginning she completely dominated her husband who was infatuated with her beauty and wit. The ceaseless intrigues that the queen fomented were at times almost incredible. Much energy was wasted in efforts to gain control in the Mediterranean so that her sons would be assured of thrones. In 1735 she at last achieved recognition of her son Charles as king of the Two Sicilies.

The closing years of Philip V's reign found Spain once more embroiled in war, this time the War of the Austrian Succession

(1740–1748). At the death of Charles VI all the earlier contenders for the Spanish throne found themselves eagerly seeking more territory. Isabel Farnesio, true to her usual driving ambition, pushed Spain into the war seeking certain Italian territories held by Austria. England and Austria lined up against Spain and France in what was a long, generally indecisive conflict. With the death of Philip in 1746 and the ascension of Ferdinand VI to the Spanish throne the desire for peace, especially in Spain, became overwhelming. The treaty two years later was greatly favorable to the aims of Isabel. Culminating nearly thirty years of repeated efforts, the peace treaty gave Spain most of the Italian possessions Isabel had coveted. The gains in Italy were for the most part offset by losses elsewhere, notably in the American colonies. While the queen had succeeded, her victory was rather a Pyrrhic one. Seeds of discontent were sown particularly in the foreign possessions that would grow into greater problems as the century passed. Isabel Farnesio, although achieving apparently glorious ends in the Mediterranean, ultimately caused results that were substantially detrimental to the Spanish state.

The reign of Ferdinand VI was much shorter than the previous one. Only thirteen years in duration, it brought something new to Bourbon Spain — peace. Ferdinand turned his attention to important matters for the real development of Spain. He was especially concerned with economic improvements and busied himself with innovative measures both at home and abroad. In seeking to modernize the government he pursued a variety of policies. The growing bureaucratic tendencies worried him, and he insisted on a streamlining of agencies. The evolution of the secretariats in a sensible, organized manner received much impetus from him. Eventually there were five of these agencies including state, war and finance, justice, navy, and the Indies. Their directors came to be called ministers, and as time passed other modern ministries appeared. Under Ferdinand these ministries were given much liberty and initiative.

Ferdinand's own personal habits also affected certain facets of Spanish life. He was a domestic person and preferred the atmosphere of his home and family. Fond of music, he introduced the custom of frequent concerts, operas, and theatrical performances into the family life at court. This interest in the arts had profound effects on their cultivation by the populace. The king's interest extended into literary and philosophical areas as well. We thus find him providing social and political protection to an increasingly besieged Feijoo, whose struggles we shall examine in the next chapter.

Ferdinand's reign was one of peace and internal development, two things that were not apparent in Philip's day. Many of the achievements, although less outwardly glorious perhaps, were actually much more solid and long-lasting. Their strength provided both permanence and brilliance to many of the great accomplishments of Ferdinand's successor.

Charles III came to the throne in 1759 at the death of his half-brother. Isabel Farnesio thus provided Spain with probably that country's greatest king ever and through his reign the highest point culturally and politically the nation achieved after the Golden Age. Charles had been king of Naples (Two Sicilies) before coming to Spain. During his rule there and in Spain he constantly sought to modernize the governments and better the state of the people. His achievements in Spain were formidable, and it is in regard to his domestic visions and realizations that he is most lauded today. There are two negative factors, however, that dull the permanent luster of his deeds. First were his entanglements in foreign wars. Second was his death in 1788 just before the French Revolution with its eventual political change all over Europe. Over the latter Charles obviously had no control.

Charles' basic problem was his opposition to England. This was not the result of some sort of paranoia but rather England's growing influence in Europe and America. Under Philip V we saw how the Spanish government was involved in war with England. Even under the peaceful Ferdinand relations were not always cordial. The principal cause of the two countries' problems lay in the English ambition to increase her colonial empire and to establish the richest commerce in the world. These related desires had been at the basis of English politics since the beginning of the seventeenth century and the founding of Jamestown. The still-strong Spanish government of the first half of that century and the tremendous power of France in the second half prevented the hoped-for realization of these desires. In the eighteenth century the decreasing power of France and the somewhat floundering attitude of Spain, especially with regard to America, enabled England to pursue her aims much more effectively. The involvement of Charles III in his various conflicts with England can be understood in the light of a changing European political situation and should not be attributed merely to his senseless abuse of the royal prerogative.

In the face of continued affronts from England Charles entered into two treaties with France that came to be called the Family Compact. The first of these (1761) was a defensive alliance against any power that should attack either of them. The second (1762) was a defensive and offensive alliance aimed directly at England. The Seven Years War thus became a reality. Although peace — greatly detrimental to Spain — was supposedly made in 1763, Spain and France considered it more as a truce, for England was more powerful than ever. Even more ominous was the jealous, vengeful attitude of the Bourbon nations because of their losses. The ever-present desire to regain lost territory naturally did not presage any continuing peace either in Europe or America. With the outbreak of revolution in the English colonies France and Spain thought the time propitious for the resumption of hostilities. Fortunately or unfortunately, depending on one's viewpoint, they could never agree on when hostilities should actually begin between England and themselves. As it was, Spain began sending supplies and munitions to the Americans as early as 1776 by way of New Orleans. By the treaty of 1783 Spain recouped some of her losses earlier in the century. Charles' government also showed a new interest in America, especially in developing relations with the United States.

When Charles III died in December, 1788, he had made Spain a first-rank nation once again. His most salient successes were in the social, economic, and political spheres. The first two areas of reforms were of a much more permanent nature, and it is for these that Spain will always be indebted to this most intelligent and enlightened of her rulers. In the last area his accomplishments were evanescent. His successor was hardly worthy of him, and, what was even worse for Spain, a new France under Napoleon was to change completely the face of Charles III's Europe.

Had Charles IV been a more competent ruler, at least some of the calamities of his reign would not have occurred. In the beginning he had excellent ministers. Floridablanca, a holdover from Charles III, was one of the best ministers of state Spain had in the eighteenth century. When in 1792 his royalist stance, however, was too much of a burden to the government in its dealings with the French, he was dismissed. He was succeeded by the very able Aranda, who unfortunately held his position for less than a year. A victim of palace intrigue as well as the complex relations with France, he was followed by Manuel Godoy, a twenty-five-year-old soldier of the royal guard. He was a man of talent, the degree of which has yet to be fully appreciated, and had much driving ambition. The principal reason for his unusual political elevation was most likely due less to his intellectual and diplomatic potential than to his being the lover of the queen, María Luisa.

In his post during most of the 1790s and into the early 1800s he attempted to achieve the best results politically for Spain. Because of the volatile situation in France and an ever-growing dislike of him at home, his position remained a difficult one. During the approximately fifteen years he was minister, Spain was forced to follow a narrow road between the interests of France and England. The ever-changing ambitions of France, especially after the supremacy of Napoleon in 1799, were greatly responsible for the changing alliances of Spain. By the beginning of the new century Spain was forced to state her alliances definitively. In 1804 war against England was declared; and the Spanish and French navies were defeated next year in the battle of Trafalgar. Godoy, although never really trusting him, sought an alliance with Napoleon, who at first duped Godoy into fighting Portugal. The Spaniards were triumphant, but none of the gains promised by Napoleon ever materialized. In fact, French troops continued to pour into northern Spain all during 1807. Godoy belatedly recognized Napoleon's ulterior motives and wished to declare war on France. Charles IV, as weak-willed as ever, opposed this idea. In the ensuing quandary Charles decided to abdicate and did so on March 19, 1808. His reasons were motivated also by the increasing popularity of his son, Ferdinand VII, who was openly courted by Napoleon.

Napoleon had not expected the abdication, and had intended to get rid of both father and son at the most propitious moment. Uncertain, oddly enough, as to exactly what course to follow, he alternately let it be known that he would restore Charles IV or would set up one of his own brothers as king of Spain. Ironically, Charles gave him his solution by secretly retracting his abdication and placing himself entirely in the power of the French. At this same time, the French general Murat suggested to Ferdinand that he go to Burgos to meet Napoleon who, he said, was coming to see him. Incredibly, although with some reluctance it must be admitted, Ferdinand went all the way across the border to Bayonne when Napoleon did not appear earlier. In Bayonne he did at last find Napoleon, who informed him that he must abdicate. As if this sad state of affairs were not enough, Charles IV, María Luisa, and Godoy also arrived and a horrendous quarrel among the royal family ensued. Both father and son were forced to abdicate and Napoleon was given the right to name Spain's new king.

The only uplifting note in this entire sorry episode concerned events in Madrid. When certain members of the royal family were forced to leave for France on the morning of May 2, 1808, the populace defied the French troops there and caused a rebellion which lasted for several hours. These events of the *Dos de mayo* signaled a national uprising against the French that continued off and on for the next six years.[2]

II *Important Ministers*

The eighteenth century was a period of both significant reforms and reformers. In Spain the most notable changes occurred in the reign of Charles III. Quite rightly he is called the most enlightened ruler Spain ever had. Yet this is not to say that Charles alone wrought these changes. His ministers were responsible for much of the forward-looking attitude in this time. Among these ministers are several in particular who deserve mention for contributions to the betterment of Spanish life.

As mentioned previously, the governmental machinery itself began to change during this century, generally to a more modern, efficient way of carrying on its business. The ministry of state evolved naturally into the most powerful of the government's agencies and usually it was these ministers of state or prime ministers who put their names to the reforms of a given time. In the first part of the century several of them were of foreign birth, usually French. Others were of Italian and Dutch origin. In 1726 the period of outstanding ministers of native birth began.

The first of these was José Patiño, who was especially important for his financial reforms. He also improved Spain's foreign commerce. Concurrent with this direction of his interests, he improved the Spanish navy and army. One of his successors was Zenón de Somodevilla, a man of quite humble birth who became the marquis of La Ensenada. It is by this name he is more generally remembered today. He was in power from 1743 to 1754. During this time he continued reforms in the same directions as those earlier carried out by Patiño. His efforts toward the upgrading of the navy were especially outstanding. When he fell from power in 1754 as the result of a disagreement with Ferdinand VI, the English are said to have rejoiced, since they felt that the Spanish navy would no longer be increased.

Still, it was in the reign of Charles III and in the early part of Charles IV's that the greatest reformers appeared. Like his forebear Philip V, Charles III brought his first ministers with him. One of the most remembered was Leopoldo de Gregorio, marquis of Esquilache, who, because of certain attempted reforms, set off the short-lived rebellion called the *motín de Esquilache* in 1766. While he is often unfairly remembered today for simply trying to change the Spaniards' mode of dress, his reforms were much needed and affected fundamental aspects of daily life.

More successful ministers of Charles III were the counts of Aranda and Floridablanca. The former (Pedro Pablo Abarca de Bolea) sought reforms in nearly all facets of Spanish life. We shall consider him later in connection with his efforts to bring about changes in the national theater. He was of a distinguished Aragonese noble family. An intelligent and intellectual man, he was at the same time obstinate and aggressive. In addition to his sensible foreign policies, he did much for the domestic scene. Ever an orderly, disciplined person, he insisted on order and discipline in the capital city and made Madrid for the first time worthy of its elevated political and social status.

Even more outstanding was José Moñino, a Murcian who was given the title of the count of Floridablanca. He embodied many of the best ideals of the enlightened gentleman and was responsible for some of the most enlightened reforms of the century. He was an honorable, intelligent, and just individual. His actions were notable in the field of improved communications in the nation — everything from roads, bridges, and canals to better and faster transportation of people, materials, and the mail. In regard to commerce, his most liberal achievement was the free-trade decree of 1778 by which Spain abandoned certain aspects of her monopolistic policy toward her colonies.

Other ministers of note were Campomanes, Jovellanos, and Godoy. Pedro Rodríguez, count of Campomanes, was from Asturias and, like others of these men, of humble birth. (It is interesting to note how through worth and ability in a supposedly class-conscious society these men could move up into extraordinarily high positions.) He labored constantly for the social and economic betterment of his country. A fascinating commentary about him was his determined royalism. This embodiment of the most ideal, enlightened concept of despotism is found in an originally poor man who strove for a better system of communications, for more industry and commerce, and for popular technical education.

Gaspar Melchor de Jovellanos, whom we shall see in various capacities, was a notable minister under Charles IV. Unfortunately, because of intrigue he was not very long in power. Yet his desire to change the status quo was lifelong. In fact, most of his reforms are contained in treatises that he wrote at different times. The important thing about Jovellanos as a man and as a government official was his tenacious search for the betterment of the Spanish people. Even though his actual time in power was short, the long-range effect of his ideas and writings was memorable. Coupled with his realistic hopes for human melioration was his idealistic determination to see things done. We find in him the zealous reformer and the eternal dreamer, the traits of several other writers and reformers of the late eighteenth century. Jovellanos reached a certain public prominence that others of these dreamers did not achieve. In him we find personified a splendid enlightened idealism combined with sensitive eighteenth-century pragmatism. In the words of John Polt, Jovellanos was "a man who was pious without superstition, patriotic without chauvinism, loyal in friendship, compassionate of the sufferings of his fellowmen, seeking always to serve others, never himself. He believed that we are social beings; and he held high standards of a citizen's duty, with which his talents and inclinations coincided to an unusually felicitous degree. Ultimately, this figure of a man whose life was dedicated to truth, utility, and virtue is Jovellanos's greatest work. For those who come to know it, its nobility is undeniable, and its attraction, irrresistible."[3]

We have mentioned Manuel Godoy when speaking of Charles IV. Because of the time in which he lived and the somewhat unsavory side of his connection to the royal family, he has often been misjudged. I think that he should be viewed a bit more sympathetically if we are to understand the significance of his public role. The fact that he was able to stay in power for so long, and in spite of the inevitable jealousies that his status engendered, is in itself a strong recommendation. He was young, and in many ways this was his weakness, because he at times thought the eagerness and charm of youth could get him through the most difficult of situations. Quite often they did. Too many times, however, they merely gave fuel to the fire of his critics. To see facets of his nature other than those self-seeking ones usually attributed to him by his enemies we have only to look at his relations with some contemporary writers. Meléndez Valdés, who may be considered a sort of Spanish poet laureate of the late 1700s, had much advice for him in his more philosophical poems. In these works Meléndez never hesitates to tell Godoy what course of action he should adopt. The former's attitude would hardly have been acceptable to a foppish, selfish, vapid individual — which is precisely how Godoy has been, and still is, portrayed.

In the following lines not only do Meléndez' admonitions stand out, but the personality of Godoy is successfully described. These lines come from Meléndez' first epistle written in 1795 and were included in the 1797 edition of his poems:

> Even more than protector, be the firm shield
> Of those who follow, prince, the steps [of art. . . .]
> The pleasing rain, the liquid dew,
> All work for the common good,
> And show the power of the great Being.
> Thus a wiser minister seeks the universal good
> Of his people who in turn trust
> In his wisdom and provident kindness.
> He directs all his actions to this good. . . .
> While the people he rules, fortunate,
> Acclaim him father. . . .[4]

Meléndez is speaking to a man who has listened to the voice of the people before and who can do so again and again. The implications of the poet's address to Godoy are significant. For too long scholars have sought the personality of Goday in the comments of those contemporaries who were prejudiced against him and in the many critics who have written about him later. The soul of this man is rather to be found in the reactions of the more sensitive authors of the period. Looking at the paternalistic portrayal of him by Meléndez we are closer to the true Godoy — a man of some vision, a man of the Enlightenment, who was unfortunately thwarted in most of his more extraordinary visions for the Spanish people. Had he lived earlier in the century he might today be remembered more sympathetically like some of his best predecessors, such as Floridablanca or Aranda. Godoy is himself an ironic figure, one among many that followed the illustrious reign of Charles III. It is an unhappy circumstance that his brilliance was wasted by a fatuous family in what were indeed rather fatuous times.

III *Government and Church*

In other European countries by the 1700s the church (whether Catholic or Protestant) had for the most part been relegated to a secondary station. Through fragmentation and civil war the Catholic church was no longer the universal institution it had been until about 1500. In Spain the church was always closely wedded to the state. The Spanish state had throughout the sixteenth and seventeenth centuries gone to war to defend the principles of the mother church. It is widely thought that many of Spain's economic and political problems in this two-hundred-year period would have been fewer, if not totally lacking, had she not so staunchly defended the church. For lack of space we cannot discuss the necessity of such a direction in Spain's politics. It is clear, however, that the independence of the state from domination by the pope has been misunderstood. During the heyday of the Spanish Hapsburgs it was the throne and not Rome that had the last word in matters pertaining to government. The church may have had its own wishes, but these were not realized unless they coincided with those of the crown. It was only in the reign of the last Hapsburg, Charles II, that the church began to exert a degree of influence that it had not had before.

When Philip V came to power in 1700 he found a rather curious situation. Whereas the Spanish throne had enjoyed great power in relation to the Catholic church until about 1670, it now was much less in control of its own destiny. This situation, made even more delicate because of the obvious physical weakness of the state noticed above, created a most unpleasant atmosphere in which to govern. While other states in the previous century had at last extricated themselves from any odious connection with the church, Spain had gone from a quite liberal relation to the church to one of servitude. Therefore, one of the first objectives of Philip was to bring about the total withdrawal of the church from participation in the government. His object was the achievement of an absolutism comparable to that of Louis XIV. The Bourbon monarchs must be understood in their determination to fashion a state that had not really ever existed in Spain before. The church, especially with its new-found gains, was not at all in favor of the directions the government began to take. Neither were the people in full accord with these directions. Nevertheless, the crown was destined to attempt an enlightened independence, and this in many ways was deservedly successful. The conflict with the church began even before Philip ascended to the throne, because the pope favored Philip's rival, the Archduke Charles. During the War of the Spanish Succession many strictures were applied by Spain against the church, only to be repealed upon termination of the conflict. In the entire reign of Philip neither the state nor the church was satisfied with the other. This was a consequence of the state's determination to follow its own course at whatever cost.

It was not until the reign of Ferdinand VI that some sort of peace between the contenders could be seen. Although Ferdinand as a man was peace-loving, in the realm of government he determined to have independence, but at a certain cost to the church's privileges. He was a devout Catholic, but in a concordat with the pope in 1753 he upheld the authority of the crown. He obtained a recognition of the royal right of patronage in appointments to most church offices. Several kinds of papal taxes were renounced as well as other churchly perquisites that established the authority of the Bourbons.

Nevertheless, the proponents of royal authority were still not satisfied. When Charles III ascended the throne the rivalry between the church and the government became increasingly apparent. The first clash occurred when the Spanish Inquisition attempted to condemn a book by a French theologian. The king replied with orders in 1761 and 1762 to the following effect: that no papal bull or other pontifical letter should be allowed to circulate or be obeyed unless it should have earlier been presented to the king so that a decision might be made as to whether it interfered with the crown's authority; that the Inquisition should publish only those edicts that were forwarded to it by the king; and that it should condemn no book without giving the author a chance to defend himself.

Numerous measures were enacted to place the Spanish clergy under the control of the king. To a great degree, these new measures were successful. The results were various. A favoring of civil courts usually occurred when they and the ecclesiastical courts came into conflict. A vigilance was imposed upon the bishops to see that members of the clergy did not speak ill of the government or the royal family. There was a limitation on the rights of asylum in churches and the personal immunities of churchmen. Ecclesiastical judges were forbidden to handle the temporal aspects of matrimonial cases. In 1787 the jurisdiction of ecclesiastical courts over all cases of smuggling was taken away, even though churchmen might be involved.

It was only natural that the Inquisition itself should come in for additional criticism and eventually a reduction in its power. The main problem with the Inquisition was its rivalry with the throne. Basically the religious body was accused of using its authority to further its political aims. In such situations it was thought that the body purposely went against the desires of the king. During the reign of Charles III when the greatest activity occurred against all arms of the church the government became more and more rigorous in its reactions to the Inquisition. In Naples Charles had shown himself to be an enemy of the Inquisition and he was not to change when he became king of Spain. In 1770 many of the cases of a secular character were removed from inquisitorial jurisdiction, and in 1784 it was ruled that all cases against the nobles had to be submitted to the crown.

At times the Inquisition rallied and tried to show its former strength. Cases against Tomás de Iriarte and Pablo de Olavide, very important figures in literary, social, and political circles, evidenced this resurgence. In general, however, the institution lost ground, and the reduction of its control continued even under Charles IV. Jovellanos and Godoy intended to abolish the body entirely, but as so often in the 1790s political events of a foreign nature prevented their actions. The Inquisition continued to exhibit its old pugnacity. Godoy was accused on three occasions of atheism, immorality, and bigamy, but the queen would not allow him to be arrested. This rather amusingly ironic action does show at least the ineffectiveness of the religious organization in the face of the crown.

The battle between the royal house and the Jesuits was even more bitter and certainly more decisive. In this conflict the throne had the support of other religious bodies that had been opposed to the Jesuit Order ever since its formation in the sixteenth century. Their hostility was based principally on jealousy, for they were envious of the dominant position of the Jesuits in church affairs and in matters of theology. This envy was not singular to Spain, because other Catholic countries at this same time were witnessing bitter opposition to the Jesuits. Adding to the opposition were the universities. They were upset because so much of the youth, especially in Spain, attended Jesuit colleges. This was especially true of the nobility from whom the leading ministers of the state were selected. The other religious orders could not abide this continuing influence of the Jesuits in the highest levels of government. If we could believe their anger was motivated from an honest interest in good government, we might be able to accept some of their fears. Unfortunately, the best interests of the state were far from their immediate concern.

Until Charles III the Bourbon kings had not actually been hostile to the Jesuit Order. By the time of his ascension in 1759 the order itself had begun to overstep its good judgment through its accumulation of great wealth. At the peak of its influence the order was psychologically ready, if we can apply such terminology to a group, for its own demise. The greatest of the Spanish kings was quite ready to help the order achieve its termination. Charles, as the enlightened and absolutist king he was, rightly feared the creeping control the Jesuits exercised over the state. The year he came to power in Spain the Jesuits were expelled from Portugal and between 1764 and 1767 from France. There were several valid reasons for their expulsion from Spain but a more emotional one is most likely what brought about the event. In both Portugal and France the Jesuits were accused of efforts to assassinate those countries' monarchs. It was not at all strange that Charles should fear similar actions against himself in Spain. When we consider his energetic nature it is not strange that he moved against the Jesuits resolutely. Thus when the famous Esquilache riots occurred in 1766, the king and his ministers used them as a pretext to evict the Jesuits whom they accused of fomenting the civil strife. The intricacies of the expulsion were many and often came close to the incredible, but after much debate a decree of expulsion was promulgated on February 27, 1767. The count of Aranda, ever the wily politician, was charged with carrying it out. He did so with such great secrecy that the Jesuits were totally surprised by the efficiency of the order. There were 2,746 Spanish Jesuits in 120 institutions scattered through 117 towns. In the New World the decree was effected in 1767 and 1768. Here there was some popular resistance to the expulsion, but not in Spain. It will be remembered that the Jesuits had been active in the Spanish colonization.

The expelled Jesuits were sent to Italy for the most part. No planning nor in fact any warning to the pope of the Jesuits' arrival was made. What we have then is the descent of many hundreds of exiles upon Italy with literally no place to go. The pope, while sympathetic to their plight, did not want them for fear of their possible interference with his own political plans. He refused to allow them entrance into the mainland. Their ships then went to Corsica where they were able to land, along with the Jesuits from America. Eventually the pope did allow them to settle in Bologna and Ferrara. Here too the exiles met with the disfavor of the other religious orders that feared them. We can understand the political reasons for the events, but it is a little difficult to accept the cruelty imposed upon these men who in general were rarely guilty of the supposed crimes of which they were accused.

Having disposed of the Jesuit problem, Charles set about to bring the church into line in other ways. One of his most notable attempts was to reduce the tremendous wealth of the church. Its revenues received from numerous sources were extraordinary, and the king understandably wished to divert this wealth into the state treasury. Although he pursued various avenues in his efforts to relieve the church of some of its financial perquisites, he was only partially successful. Supposedly he did increase the government's coffers with the confiscation of Jesuit property and financial resources after 1767. However, nothing definite can really be ascertained on this matter. With all the efforts of the Bourbons by the end of the century the church was still very wealthy. It has been estimated that its annual income reached nearly seventy million dollars.

The other main point of attack was the reduction of the clergy itself. Here again we can only be amazed — Chapman estimates one churchman to every five to ten adult men in 1787.[5] This large number alone made possible much vice and immorality. Both the government and the *Ilustrados* attacked this aspect of the church, with varying degrees of success. In general, however, we find the church was better in remedying its own problems than at any previous time. This constant effort at internal reform and the determined desire of the monarchy to bring the church under control characterize the church as a much more modern, humane institution than it had ever been.

IV *Economics*

Closely related to the question of state and church is that of economics. As we have seen, the church drained much money from the state. This loss of revenue caused the government many problems that it might not otherwise have experienced. But even aside from the government's problems with the church it was the basic economic position of the country that inspired all the great reforms of the eighteenth century in Spain. We must remember once more that on entering the 1700s the country was suffering in this area as in all others. By 1700 Spain did not have the European political hegemony enjoyed until approximately 1650. Without this supremacy she could no longer override some of her essential economic woes that had always lain dormant, only waiting for the proper moment to flare up. It is those economic difficulties and the efforts to remedy them that we shall briefly note here.

At the beginning of the century Spain had some six million inhabitants. By 1787 this figure had almost doubled. The growth would seem to indicate a healthy, comfortable citizenry, but such was not nearly the case. Of the later population figure nearly a third of the total was clergy, nobles (by far the most numerous of this third), and those who served them. This extraordinary proportion, or disproportion, was at the basis of the overall economic problems. Farmers and laborers accounted for nearly two million people. This fact indicates that by the end of the century Spain was still essentially an agrarian society with only a small percentage of merchants. After all the reforms, especially those of Charles III, the existing situation illustrates how very terrible must have been that at the beginning of the century, making evident the tremendous need for reform that greeted the new Bourbon rulers and the early *Ilustrados*.

The general domestic scene helps us to better understand the plight of the ordinary citizens and their rulers in trying to help them. By the end of the century the economic and resulting domestic problems were still severe. Aragon and old Castile were in miserable shape, hardly living up to their agricultural potential. Such regions as La Mancha were in a far worse condition. The character of Spanish houses of many ordinary citizens further helps our understanding of the economic situation. Cave houses and adobe huts with straw roofs existed in Castile. The houses of Galicia were portrayed as having walls of stone placed together without cement, hardly higher than a man's height, with great chunks of rock for roofs. The doorway and a hole in the roof served as the only means of light and the outlet for smoke. The hygienic conditions were obviously deplorable, particularly when one considers that barn animals made use of the same abode. Before we criticize, however, we should recall that we are talking of a situation two hundred years ago when the hygiene we know today was still undreamed of. Nor was it uncommon to use whatever materials were at hand for house construction. We Americans of log-cabin fame should be distinctly aware of this.

The really unfortunate aspect of the above situation consisted of the illiteracy and ignorance of the common people, even though this was much the same in France, Germany, England, and the English colonies. The essential difference between the Spanish and English colonies abroad was the superior social mobility in the English colonies existent especially after the American Revolution. In Spain economic inequality arose from the ownership by a few families of vast landed estates, from the difficulty of communications, the great burdens of taxation, the mismanagement of certain bureaucracies, the many wars, and — something particularly Spanish — from a persistent dislike of manual labor.[6]

One of the worst results of the bad economic situation was the hordes of beggars that roamed the cities and countryside. During the reign of Charles III many efforts were made to reduce the numbers of these unfortunate people. The efforts were in the humanitarian spirit of Charles' enlightened rule. Physically able women were given work in workshops or, perhaps more correctly, "state shops." Men were enrolled in the army and navy, and old and sick people were placed in homes for the aged or in hospitals. Often the lack of funds prevented a complete implementation of these worthy schemes. The goals were similar to those of our own New-Deal programs, and it would seem the plans had the approbation of the most idealistic people of the times. Another quotation from Meléndez is apt here. In his *Discursos forenses* he wrote:

I believe that only a charitable association can carry out the important task of caring for the poor ... an association that is authorized by the most illustrious faction in the capital ... and the best people in the lowliest of towns. It would be an organization decorated with civil honors and sanctified with the church's approbation.... [Among the association's principal functions would be] the listing and classifying of the poor and needy of the provinces ... the distribution of alms to all according to their needs ... the establishment of a method for this distribution ... the bringing together of all beggars and vagabonds on a specified day in order to disperse them among various charitable institutions or return them to their native villages ... to carry out the same action in regard to orphans ... to provide work for them and prohibit forever afterward beggary and vagrancy with the severest punishments ... to prohibit with the same severity all public almsgiving in the street since it produces only more idleness ... and finally to interest public opinion in this great undertaking. And how many more objectives could such an association not undertake...? Would it be far-fetched for it to send these beggars into the country to till the fields? Could the government not lend its aid in establishing these unfortunate people in the many underpopulated areas we have? Could not these people plant the many thousands of trees we need and assure the harvest with irrigation...?[7]

By far the most energetic economic reforms came not from the government but from groups of private individuals. These local organizations, the Sociedades Económicas de los Amigos del País (Economic Societies of Friends of the Country), even in their name proved their altruistic, humanitarian, and nationalistic aims. The first society was formed by a Basque nobleman, the count of Peñaflorida, when he returned from France with the intention of organizing a learned society or *salon* on the order of those so popular in France. Although much activity went on before 1764, it was in this year that Peñaflorida and fifteen other Basque noblemen sought permission from the government to start an official organization. Permission was granted in 1765. From this time on the popularity of the organization permeated other sections of the nation and more societies were founded. The focus of the groups was the betterment of the economic situation. To effect any change the members knew that there were other aspects of the government and society that had to be altered as well. It was not long before the organizations took up programs dealing with matters not immediately linked to the economy. Thus from their encouragement of agriculture, industry, and commerce they quickly progressed to open cultivation of the arts and sciences. They soon had permission to establish institutions to instruct pupils in Latin, French, geography, Spanish history, and experimental physics. The Basque Society, for example, "to further the local economy ... ordered linen seed from Riga, supported a knife factory, offered one thousand reales for a memoir on the best kind of blacksmith's bellows, and built up a library at Vergara of Spanish and foreign works of a practical nature." In their first meeting papers were read and an oral examination of students followed. We see quite well the essentially didactic purpose of the societies. Perhaps no other group of the Spanish eighteenth century illustrates so well that period's determination to overcome stagnation through research, teaching, and examination.[8]

Other plans and projects, often of a utopian character, were effected. To reclaim much of the wasted cropland of Spain the government backed many schemes. The most famous of these was its attempt to people uninhabited lands of the southern portion of the country. Foreign colonists were brought from Germany, since this sort of reclamation had been particularly successful in some Catholic German states. In 1767 a royal charter was drawn up by Campomanes giving instructions for the settlement of deserted areas along the principal highway from Madrid to Seville and Cádiz, in the Sierra Morena, and between Córdoba and Seville. Land, houses, animals, and farm implements were given to the settlers in return for rent paid to the government. To prohibit the growth of large landholdings the colonists could not mortgage, increase, or divide their property. Except for parish churches all religious institutions were kept out. Direction of the grand project was given to Pablo de Olavide, who came under attack by the Inquisition and in 1776 was imprisoned. This setback did not help the settlements, which eventually did number forty-four villages and eleven flourishing towns in an area of some one thousand square miles. This truly awesome project — the fact that it ever existed is an accolade for Charles III's government — was the most successful agricultural plan Spain attempted. Other similar ones were intended for Extremadura, but they never materialized.[9]

Public works appeared on a vast scale, again especially in the reign of Charles III. The construction of irrigation canals was begun, but many were never completed or were constructed so poorly that they were not long in use. Great highways were planned and some of them were completed. An efficient mail service was inaugurated by Floridablanca. Government support was given the shipbuilding industry and other commercial ventures. A national bank was established under Charles III but failed under his successor. Yet the government did try to hold itself a bit aloof from its old habit of regulating manufacturing. A new sort of laissez-faire attitude developed under Charles III. This, joined with the government's general educative measures such as the establishment of model factories, brought about a certain revival of industrial life. In the implementation of new policies many foreigners were invited to come to Spain and assist in their development.[10] Many others came on their own. What resulted was a rather large number of policy-making decisions made by foreigners. As would be expected, this situation was not very popular with the general mass of the population and was yet one more reason for the increasing anti-French attitude of the people. By no means was this "invasion" bad, for such distinguished people as Bernardo Ward, an Irishman who settled in Spain and became a royal official of Ferdinand VI, did much good for Spain.

In all this activity what we note most is the variety of extraordinary projects carried out, though not always successfully, by the state and by private citizens. Both were inspired by the need to update Spain's economic outlook and well-being. This same variety of endeavors too helps us to comprehend the fervor with which the enlightened leaders and ordinary citizens determined to bring about change in their country. That their activities were not always understood and accepted by the people should not be construed as a fault of the *Ilustrados*. The fact that they attempted a better world merits the appreciation of all who have had interest in the welfare of Spain.

V   *Learned Societies*

We have mentioned the phenomenon of the economic societies. The direction of these was intellectual at times but, as stated above, their primary object was the improvement of economic and social life. There were other organizations, specifically intellectual, that were determinedly cultural in their purposes. The first and most important of these was the Spanish Royal Academy. It owed its formation to the efforts of the marquis of Villena, Juan Manuel Fernández Pacheco, who held political and military posts under both Charles II and Philip V. Under the latter Villena became viceroy of Sicily and Naples. When he returned to Spain in 1711, he had already become an ardent admirer of Italian institutions. One especially was the Academy of La Crusca in Florence. The interests of this academy in the language and even more so those of the French Academy founded in 1635 by Richelieu led the marquis to strive for a similar establishment in Spain.

On August 3, 1713, the Royal Academy was formally instituted with its main function that of compiling a dictionary of the Spanish language. Villena was elected president. Quite soon the elected members, among whom were some of the most important literary figures of the time, set to work on what would be a long, arduous task. In their labors the members relied particularly on Covarrubias' outstanding seventeenth-century work, *Tesoro de la lengua castellana* (*Thesaurus of the Spanish Language*). To amplify its and their own interpretations they also relied on foreign dictionaries.

The principal difference between the dictionaries of the Spanish and French Academies is the former's flexibility and its lack of dogmatic rigidity. A good indication is its inclusion of dialectical terms from all regions of Spain. The first volume appeared in 1726 and the remaining five in 1729, 1732, 1734, 1737, and 1739. These years of publication have a curious correspondence to those of Feijoo's *Teatro crítico universal* (*Universal Theater of Criticism*), which we shall view in our next chapter.

The academy also undertook the publication of a treatise on *Orthography* (1742) and a *Grammar* on which work was begun in 1740 but which did not see publication until 1771. The significant thing in all these works, as well as in the formation of the academy itself, is the realization in Spain that the time had come to set up norms, to stabilize and guide the language, albeit quietly. This attitude is basic to the entire century, and we shall see it time and time again in many varied ways.

The Academy of History began in 1735 with meetings by a group of learned men. Its members were interested in literary as well as historical matters, and it is in great part from the crystallization of the first members' interests that later investigative works of import came about. At first their direction was not too clear, not even to themselves, but as time passed they divided themselves up according to their preferred interests such as history in general, geography of the ancient world, modern geography, natural history, primitive languages, religion, genealogy, inscriptions, and many others. Their interests corresponded nicely with those of the antiquarian societies in England during this century. Of interest to us as Americans is Benjamin Franklin's election to the Spanish Academy of History in 1784, the first American to be so honored.[11]

Of a slightly different character but just as important as the two just discussed was the Royal Library founded in 1712 by Philip V. Its establishment was extremely significant for the history of Spanish literature. At first it was dependent on the contents and funds of the "Library of the Queen Mother," but soon it was receiving copies of all books and pamphlets published by Spanish presses. This resembled the foundation of the British Museum library from the collection of George III.

Mention should be made of less formal gatherings that, while not incorporated as were the above, did nevertheless exert great influence on the intellectual life in Spain during the eighteenth century. The two most famous were the Academia del Buen Gusto (Academy of Good Taste) and the Tertulia de la Fonda de San Sebastián (Tertulia of the Inn of Saint Sebastian). The first was of relatively short duration (1749–1751). It met in the palace of the countess of Lemos. Many of the original members were of the nobility. Of those remembered today probably the most notable was Ignacio de Luzán. His membership indicates in itself the essentially neoclassic attitude of the group. The Academia was therefore greatly responsible for aiding the spread of neoclassic literary doctrine in the middle of the century.

The Tertulia was even more rigid in its adherence to neoclassic tenets. Its members met regularly in the inn of the group's name. Its formation was in many ways an attempt to continue the efforts of the Academia del Buen Gusto, and with this conscious attempt at imitation it was natural for it to be a little more strict in its goals. In their gatherings the members read their newly written works to each other, criticizing their efforts. The friendship and affability of the group was extraordinary, and because of the members' candor and the resultant free atmosphere, some of the best literary work of the century was produced.

Other *salons* existed in Spain. All in all they manifest the spirit of regeneration that runs through the 1700s. The spontaneity, at times cloaked in a certain decorous neoclassic wrap, of these groups and the valuable productions they engendered are a good testimony to the individual spirit of vitality and exuberance that reigned among Spain's intellectuals. It is perhaps a little difficult to imagine such groups today when "artistic" organizations must often have the financial backing of the government to function. The Tertulia did have the favor of Charles III's enlightened government, but it was more a sort of benevolent approval than anything else.

VI   *Polemics*

The last section of this chapter must deal with a somewhat different matter. While arguments themselves do not stand out like movements or inscriptions they nevertheless can have lasting effects. Polemics were a very important aspect of cultural life in eighteenth-century Europe. Spain was no exception. As a result quite a few literary works came from the public and private verbal wrangling of her literati. We shall see that while the arguments in themselves were not necessarily of enduring significance, some of the works they produced were. These works in certain cases influenced literary development substantially. It is satire that was the basic note of eighteenth-century Spanish literature. Through biting criticism, and even ridicule, writers knew they could call attention to what they considered abuses. The power of the written word thus became influential as a device for the destruction, the reconstruction, and the regeneration of ideas. As an essential part of literary production the polemic has probably never had such widespread cultivation. To be sure, with Quevedo in the seventeenth, Larra in the nineteenth, and the Generation of '98 in the nineteenth and twentieth centuries, we find this literary form cultivated to the fullest degree. But it was in the 1700s that the polemic attained its maximum effect.

We shall examine three manifestations of the polemical attitude, each quite different from the other and each quite public and popular in its time. The first derives from an important publication that unfortunately enjoyed too short a lifespan, the *Diario de los literatos de España* (*Diary of the Writers of Spain*). It was in this journal that the polemic really had its origin; the ideas expressed in it were a new venture in the literary sphere. The journal first appeared in 1737, by coincidence, perhaps, also the date of Luzán's *Poética* (*Poetics*). The *Diary* was edited by Francisco Manuel de Huerta, Juan Martínez Salafranca, and Leopoldo Jerónimo Puig. Its purpose was to express an opinion of the value of all the books that were printed in Spain. The opinions expressed would elicit either favorable or unfavorable reaction from the public. Very quickly the desire to provide a simple review of new publications turned into a war against bad taste in literature. Adverse criticism against the contributors and their reviews soon appeared. The *Diary* was forced to interrupt publication after its fifth number. Only with the publicized assistance of Philip V was it able to continue and then for just two more issues. The contributors were becoming in their reviews just as pugnacious as their detractors. The verbal battle was soon to reach a climax, and this caused the journal's demise in 1742.

Robert E. Pellisier expresses a judgment on the failure of the *Diary*. He suggests that its demise had a truly unfortunate effect on the progress of the neoclassic movement of reform in Spain.[12] Until this time the arguments between reformers and antireformers had essentially been based on logic and usually a sense of fair play.

From this time on, however, the combatants made the quarrel a sort of nationalistic one. That is, the reformers in their attempts to change ideas and practices were seen as opposing a national literature and as favoring foreign works and models. Those who advocated change were thus labeled as seditious. This unhappy development in the thought processes of the literati, which would extend into all levels of society, continued throughout the century. This jingoistic bent was responsible essentially for the antireform attitude that triumphed in the nineteenth century with Menéndez y Pelayo's defense of such people as Forner. It has continued into our own day with the still widespread rejection of the enlightened reformers' real purpose, that of molding Spanish thought with new concepts, whether from within the country or from the outside.

The second example of the polemics of the period is really a part of the *Diary.* In 1742 a work was published in the journal that would become a sort of clarion call for the reformers. This was the *Sátira contra los malos escritores de este siglo (Satire Against the Bad Writers of This Century*) by Jorge Pitillas, pseudonym for José Gerardo de Hervás. In succinct terms it tells what the new reformers intended, especially in the area of literature. Hervás in the name of good taste — and inspired by Boileau — condemned the baroque excesses of contemporary poetry and, interestingly enough, the introduction of French terms into the Spanish language. An important element of this little work was its belligerence. There is none of the moderation of Luzán, for example. Hervás is out to destroy once and for all his enemies, as also the *Diary's,* and those of the enlightened reformers. The work as reasoned argument is not so important, but in its harshness and its popular acceptance it represents very well the continuation of both a general and a specific polemic in the century. The first of the two concerns the increasingly bitter enmity between the reformers or neoclassicists and the antireformers or traditionalists whom we shall meet again in the coming pages. The more specific polemic is that of Hervás and the *Diary* against its immediate detractors, a polemic that did not completely end with the death of the journal.

The last example we present of these seemingly inevitable polemics is a man, Juan Pablo Forner. Possessed of a highly irascible temper Forner represents the epitome of the polemical attitude of the 1700s. Living in the second half of the century, his enemies were seemingly without end, but he fought them all relentlessly. These enemies he had gained usually by himself, for his temper, naturally vituperative, alienated more people than it charmed. His most memorable arguments were with the Iriartes. We shall see Tomás de Iriarte (1750-1791) in much more detail in chapter 4. His was an extremely productive life that would probably have been even more fertile had it not been for his premature death. He was fortunate in having early access through his uncle, the erudite Juan de Iriarte, to many of the best literary *salons*. Forner, whose life was much less charmed, was very jealous of Iriarte's ease of movement. This jealousy no doubt caused much of his bitterness and provoked his long and outspoken condemnation of Iriarte.

Forner (1756-1797) came from a Valencian family of some local standing but not of sufficient power to give him the access to society he always longed for. He attended the Universities of Salamanca and Toledo but little is actually known of the extent or profundity of his studies. In 1778 he went to Madrid to work in the field of law and to live with an uncle. Except for his literary activities his life was hardly outstanding. In 1790 he was named to an official legal post in Seville and in 1796 to one in Castile. Here, in Madrid, he died in 1797. It appears that this rather lackluster civic career did not bother Forner too greatly, because his real ambition was to advance in the literary field. While he possessed little creative capacity he more than made up for this lack with his bitingly clever and sarcastic opinions. His road to renown lay quite naturally therefore in the area of the literary polemic. To choose a conspicuous and excitable target was all he needed to do. His choice in 1781 of Iriarte was a natural one.

In that year Iriarte wrote a defense of his eclogue "La felicidad de la vida del campo" ("The Happiness of Country Life"), which he had submitted to the Royal Academy competition in poetry in 1779. In this competition Iriarte's poem was awarded second place to Meléndez Valdés' eclogue, "Batilo." Iriarte was genuinely upset at the award and felt that he had been publicly maligned in having lost the first-place award, since Meléndez was virtually unknown at that time. Many critics have seized on this aspect of jealousy in Iriarte's defense of his poem, titled *Reflexiones sobre la égloga de Batilo* (*Reflections on the Eclogue Batilo*), and have roundly condemned it. There is solid judgment in the *Reflections*, and its publication aroused much attention. Forner saw his opportunity for public recognition. Professing anger at the attack on his young friend Meléndez, Forner launched into a severe diatribe against Iriarte. His pamphlet is entitled *Cotejo de las églogas que ha pre-*

miado la Real Academia de la Lengua (*Comparison of the Eclogues Awarded Prizes by the Royal Academy of the Language*). The author thus took advantage of the situation to enhance his own stature, admittedly quite inferior at this time, by expanding the debate that had so conveniently arisen.

What Forner says in the *Comparison* is essentially what he would write again and again in the next ten years. Much of the work is pertinent, but it loses value in part because of the personal hatred it reveals toward Iriarte. Forner's position is a totally negative one, and is mocking and belittling as well. Since he is directing himself against a man who was well known, it is to be expected that his diatribes might delight Iriarte's peers, who were much given to personal vituperation. Iriarte's style of writing, the "prosaic" or unpoetic quality of his verse, is the main preoccupation of Forner — and it has continued to concern critics down to our own day. At the end of his essay Forner bluntly states his feelings about Iriarte's poem and Iriarte himself. He implies that there is nothing redeeming in the poetry from the standpoint of character development, atmosphere, or message. Certainly there is nothing worthwhile in the style:

I conclude then by saying that in the work of Mr. Cisneros [Iriarte] besides there being no color or bucolic style, there is no color or universal style; that his expression is exaggerated in part, base in another, languid here, and violent there; that his personages express themselves at times like poets, at other times like very urbane people or like philosophers or politicians or hermits ... their language ... is of an elegance foreign to our poetry in which it is not always correct to introduce sentences of a prosaic style ... but ... the author will attribute all that is said here to calumny and the desire to malign....[13]

As a recent article points out, from 1781 on Iriarte became an obsession with Forner.[14] In 1782 there appeared the *Fábulas literarias* (*Literary Fables*), Iriarte's most significant contribution to letters. As we shall see in chapter 4 it was an important work not only to the neoclassic movement in Spain but to European literature as a whole. Forner wrote his own *El asno erudito* (*The Erudite Ass*) the same year, once more a virulent attack on Iriarte's work and personality. The *Literary Fables* achieved an immediate notoriety because of their supposed allusions to contemporaries. Forner thought himself portrayed unflatteringly in several of the poems, although the question of these so-called allusions has never been satisfactorily resolved. In Forner's case, his unveiled desire to achieve renown would have led him to condemn any allusion to himself, whether real or imagined, simply because he wished to hear his name bandied about in public.

Iriarte's reply to Forner's poem was his essay *Para casos tales suelen tener los maestros oficiales* (*For Just Such Cases Do They Have Trained Teachers*). This work is valuable today as a kind of prose commentary on the *Fables,* clarifying in many cases what criticisms Iriarte was making. The book is in the form of a letter to Iriarte written by Eleuterio Geta, a supposedly close friend who of course is Iriarte himself. Don Eleuterio proceeds very logically to urge Iriarte to react to Forner's malicious fable. After giving many examples of uncalled-for provocation on the part of Forner, Don Eleuterio begins to note Iriarte's purposes in writing his didactic poems. At one point he quotes from Forner's own writing to show rather ingeniously what the *Fables* really are:

"And what is the teaching they announce to us? Perhaps the intimate deli-cacies of the arts; the ways for finding the truth among so many doubts; the certain resolution of the opinions that tire human understanding so much? Not at all, not at all. These bagatelles are good only for a Doctor Gothic, or for an insipid and silly Scholastic.... They teach what they can: general, common things that anyone knows without study and there-fore without the necessity for tiring oneself in reading bad verses.... They teach, for example: *That it is better to do one thing well than many badly; That he who works without the rules of art succeeds only by chance, if he succeeds at all.... That a nicely bound book can be poorly written; That a house can have a good façade and a horrible exterior* [Iriarte's italics]. Good Lord! What new and useful discoveries for the good of man!" [Don Eleuterio, that is, Iriarte, goes on in his brilliant way to dismiss the sar-casm of the comments and to put them to his own use.] It seems ... that the delicate taste of Mr. Segarra [Forner] is not satisfied with those clear and simple truths that we read in all the philosophers, in the books of Christian ethics, and significantly in the fabulists. The moral truths of Aesop are all very natural and quite trivial....[15]

At about this time Iriarte came under attack by Félix María de Samaniego, author of the *Fábulas morales* (*Moral Fables*) who felt maligned, or rather, upstaged by the younger fabulist. Fortunately Iriarte made no reply in print, but he did attempt to have legal action brought against his adversary. Nothing came of this action except the discovery of another work by Forner, *Los gramáticos: historia chinesca* (*The Grammarians: A Chinese History*). Not only was the book a diatribe against Tomás de Iriarte but also against the memory of his uncle, Juan de Iriarte. The essay is given a Chinese setting, recalling the fascination of the Enlightenment with things Chinese. Forner is perhaps utilizing such a setting here, however, to satirize further two men who were enlightened and who were much interested in the Chinese vogue. (For example, Iriarte had earlier translated Voltaire's *The Chinese Orphan.*) The plot of the work is rudimentary. Suffice it to say that Juan de Iriarte and his nephew are given Chinese names and placed in a mythical China. Forner first accuses the uncle of gaining political influence and then of bringing in his nephews to share in it. From chapter 9 on his diatribes are directed specifically against Tomás and his brother Bernardo, reiterating the quarrels Tomás was involved in and sadistically telling what happened in each of them. In essence, Forner rather masochistically for his own part relives all their old polemics while trying to start a new one.

Forner had one more reason for writing this particular essay. He felt it time to campaign actively with government officials for the renown he so much desired. He ends his book with some very laudatory statements to the count of Floridablanca, the prime minister, and some hypocritical, self-effacing comments about himself. Floridablanca did inquire about the outspoken writer but prohibited the publication of *The Grammarians.* Nothing daunted, Forner petitioned Charles III but with no better success. *The Grammarians* had to wait until the twentieth century for its publication.[16]

The sad thing about this book is the hatred shown for the *Ilustración* and some of the *Ilustrados.* Forner rails out especially against Feijoo (as he had done on earlier occasions). Forner himself wanted change and many of his closest friends, who eventually became enemies, were *Ilustrados* of his age. The harm that Forner would do to the Spanish *Ilustración* in the works below is therefore already foretold in *The Grammarians.*

During the 1780s, the period of most activity between Iriarte and Forner, an article was published in the *Encyclopédie Méthodique* (*Encyclopedia of Method*) by a M. Masson de Morvilliers in which he wrote: "The Spaniard has the aptitude for science; he has a great many books, and, nevertheless, his nation is perhaps the most ignorant of Europe. . . . But what does one owe to Spain? And after two centuries, after four, after ten, what has she done for Europe?"[17] Masson was an unknown who would probably have remained so if Antonio José de Cavanilles, who had been in France for several years, had not taken it upon himself to vindicate the honor of his country. This vindication he undertook by publishing first in France (1784) a pamphlet that was immediately translated into Spanish and called simply *Observaciones* (*Observations*). Cavanilles gave a glowing picture of the Spain of his day and in passing mentioned Iriarte very flatteringly. The essay was well received in France. In Spain, however, it was received with a great uproar and a sort of cathartic outcry against France and her products such as M. Masson. Much was written in defense of the fatherland. Most important for us, Floridablanca subsidized a work by Forner, *Oración apologética por la España* (*Apologetic Oration for Spain*), published in 1786.

Floridablanca had remembered the earlier brashness of Forner and decided to reward him with the publication of this work. It itself has received mixed reactions in the last two hundred years, most of the favorable reception probably being based on Menéndez y Pelayo's strong approval of it. The essay defends the literature of the homeland, and herein lie its major defects. Lauding literary productions of the sixteenth and seventeenth centuries to an excessive degree, it appears to criticize contemporary writers and their works. While on the one hand it does indeed defend Spain's literature, it does very little for Spanish literature of the eighteenth century. Forner's antipathy toward the *Ilustrados* gives a negative tone to the work. Granted the possibility that Forner may not have intended to criticize the literature of his own day, he nevertheless appeared to do so. This intentional or unintentional criticism is at the heart of the negative attitude toward the reforming spirit of the 1700s that arose in the nineteenth and twentieth centuries. In many ways Forner's risible traditionalism sets literary progress back by years. Caught in the midst of the whole rather silly episode, the public found it easier to accept negative criticism of new approaches more easily than what, ostensibly, was only a defense of a great literary past.

We shall mention one final work by Forner that probably has given him his most lasting renown — the *Exequias de la lengua castellana* (*Exequies of the Spanish Language*). This was written about 1790 but was not published until after his death. The work is a commentary on outstanding Spanish writers and the literary currents Forner sees in his country's history. Yet in its biased attitude toward contemporary authors it still possesses too much of Forner's bitter, acerbic personality. As in all his other writings, Forner cannot avoid vituperation. Because he does once more laud the great writers of earlier times the work was much appreciated by the nineteenth century as it sought to assess the achievements of the preceding era. Menéndez y Pelayo more than anyone lauded Forner and his work. Thus, Forner through Menéndez y Pelayo established a view of the eighteenth-century *Ilustrados* as petty, quarrelsome, and not very visionary. The ironic note is that this view is based on the work of a writer who was perhaps the most narrow-minded and envious Spain has ever produced.

With this brief look at history, politics, and attitudes in Spain in the eighteenth century we can now turn to other literary artists who in many and varied ways determined the ambience of the period. They in themselves are often extraordinarily interesting and add much in tone and color to what is too often termed a lackluster, imitative period in Spain's literature.

CHAPTER 2

Spanish Prose of the Eighteenth Century

I   *The Beginning of the* Ilustración

IT is not only a real fact but a symbolic one as well that the Enlightenment in Spain begins with the publication of a series of didactic essays. Fray Benito Jerónimo Feijoo y Montenegro brought out the first volume of his *Teatro crítico universal* (*Universal Theater of Criticism*) in 1726. For the next several years (1726–1739) Spain would witness the appearance of eight more volumes in this series and five others in his *Cartas eruditas y curiosas* (*Intellectual Letters,* 1742–1760). The publications elicited an enormous outpouring of works by other writers, with judgments both positive and negative in their evaluation of Feijoo and his new and unusual contributions to the contemporary Spanish mentality. No other author of the century had such a lasting and definitive influence on the arts and the people as this erudite and kindly Benedictine.

Feijoo was not the first to realize the need to modernize the Spanish public's outlook on life. Neither was he the first to call for the reconciliation of religion and science. Others since the Renaissance had voiced such sentiments. By the eighteenth century this lack of "reconciliation" had become more acute and aggravated. The drastic necessity to change the nation's attitudes about the more scientifically inclined world outside could no longer be postponed or bypassed. The people in general wallowed in an apathy and provincialism that came directly from an ignorance that was now being eradicated in other European countries. As we have noted in the first chapter, there were efforts by the government in the early 1700s toward effective change in the people's life-style. All too often, however, the people feared change because it meant

45

the uncertainty of newness. To a nation fanatically imbued with a Catholic spirit that had become so deeply ingrained, especially since the days of Philip II, any attempt to introduce "foreign" methods or beliefs was often decried as traitorous and un-Christian.

Feijoo was the first to proceed in a sensible, affirmative manner to try to solve the national spiritual dilemma. Fundamentally he was a teacher who saw the best approach for resolving the matter through a teacher's sensitivity, determination, and mild prodding. It is fascinating that such an individual could affect the numbers of people and the national mentality to the degree that he did, but his was a mature and understanding nature that tended to elicit trust and acceptance.

Feijoo was born in 1676 in Galicia. At the age of fourteen he entered the Benedictine monastery of San Julián de Samos in Galicia. After nearly twenty years of study he went to teach theology at the monastery of San Vicente in Oviedo. The next year he joined the faculty of the University of Oviedo where he held the Theology Chair of Saint Thomas. He was in this position until 1721 when he was elected abbot of his monastery, which appointment he held for two years. In 1724 he was given a more senior chair of theology. The next year he went to Madrid where he busied himself with the publication of his *Universal Theater of Criticism*. In 1727 he became an honorary member of the Royal Society of Medicine of Seville, and in 1729 he was reelected abbot. He held the most senior chair of theology from 1737 until retirement in 1739. This was by no means the end of his career, since he was still to begin the publication of his *Intellectual Letters* three years later. Fernando VI honored him with the title of "Councillor" in 1748 and in 1750 issued a decree forbidding further attacks on Feijoo's books. On September 26, 1764, Feijoo died at his monastery in Oviedo.[1]

This short résumé of Feijoo's life is intended only to present the salient features of his long career. What we want to emphasize are two aspects of this career — that of teacher and that of scholar. Each is intrinsically connected to the other. If Feijoo had not been a teacher, he would never have been able to communicate with a public of varied intelligence and capacity. The simple fact that he wrote in Spanish, not in Latin as most scholars of his day, underscores the natural desire of the teacher to clarify facts and to relate them easily to his students, in this case the Spanish people. The scholarly aspect of Feijoo's life was always present. Interestingly, he was middle-aged when he began to publish. The late appearance of his work was more than adequately recompensed by its amount and diversity. He is not unlike Cervantes in this regard. While Cervantes had written novels and plays before *Don Quixote,* it was this product of his latter years that has justly given him his renown. In Feijoo's case the time that passed before the volume of the *Universal Theater of Criticism* appeared was essential in his development as a thinker and purveyor of knowledge. It was necessary — and fortunate — that he be an older man of mature judgment and sensibility if he was to give his contemporaries his own view of the world around them.

Before considering some of the ideas in the *Universal Theater* and the *Intellectual Letters,* we should note the vicissitudes Feijoo experienced during the years of their publication. His first venture into print was an essay, a *Letter* (1725) in defense of Dr. Martín Martínez' *Skeptical Medicine.* In his essay Feijoo approves of a certain amount of skepticism in every human being. Particularly on the natural or physical plane he was quite ready to reserve judgment on all theories that could not be demonstrably proved. This healthy doubting is at the basis of both of his great works. Their publication began the next year, and they too urge the public to look at old and new theories with a questioning attitude. Feijoo is not advocating the negativism and cynicism of the later French *Philosophes,* and especially not in regard to religion. Rather, he is urging his readers to think and not blindly to believe something merely because it may be presented from a pulpit, in a learned work (often in a Latin incomprehensible to the ordinary reader), or as accepted religious or political dogma or superstition. This viewpoint is one that will appear again and again in the century, whether expressed by an essayist like Feijoo, a novelist like Isla, or a poet like Iriarte.

Given the attitude of healthy doubt and criticism espoused by Feijoo, it is not unexpected that he and his works should have been the recipients of many attacks. The first really significant assault came in 1729 with the publication of Salvador José Mañer's *Antiteatro crítico (Anti-Theater of Criticism).* To this excessively meticulous critique Feijoo replied in the same year with his *Ilustración apologética (Apologetic Illustration).* Mañer published the second part of his *Anti-Theater* in 1731, in which he professed to have found 998 errors in the third volume of Feijoo's *Theater.* In 1732 Feijoo's close friend Fray Martín Sarmiento came to his defense with a rare publication of his own, *Demostración apolo-*

gética (*Apologetic Demonstration*).

Feijoo wisely decided to terminate this polemic, but there were others that immediately took its place. Because of lack of space I shall mention only the more outstanding ones. Father Francisco de Soto y Marne published his baitingly acerbic *Reflexiones crítico-apologéticas sobre las obras de Feijoo* (*Critico-Apologetic Reflections on the Works of Feijoo*, 1748–1749). Ostensibly criticism of a literary and scientific character, the two volumes were really personal diatribes that went so far as to question the seriousness of Feijoo's religious convictions. Feijoo replied with his *Justa repulsa de inicuas acusaciones* (*Just Repulse of Iniquitous Accusations,* 1749). At this point the king ordered that no more attacks on Feijoo be published. Soto y Marne sought permission from Fernando VI to publish other volumes against Feijoo, but the king held his ground.

We can also note the criticism of Father Jacinto Segura attacking Feijoo's defense of Savonarola, that of the Jesuit Joaquín Javier Aguirre because Feijoo preferred Lucan to Vergil, and that of Mayans y Siscar because Feijoo had made what Mayans felt was an erroneous and unjust criticism of him. The altercation between Feijoo and Diego de Torres Villarroel was most fascinating because of its theme. Feijoo had roundly attacked the popularity of astrological "science" in his "Astrología judiciaria y almanaques" ("Judiciary Astrology and Almanacs"). Torres, a most popular figure, as we shall see, defended astrological prognostications, since a great deal of his money and popularity came from providing them.

There were many friends and numerous defenders of Feijoo to counteract the above negative critics. We have already noted Sarmiento. Fernando VI's protection shows the monarchy's interest in Feijoo as a human being and especially in the nurturing of the advancement of scientific knowledge. Charles III continued to praise him and even presented him with important archaeological treasures from Herculaneum, whose excavation had begun under his sponsorship.[2]

These polemics were unfortunate for Feijoo in some ways, and yet they motivated him to produce even more than he might originally have planned. They show us today the extraordinary daring and courage of one man who almost single-handedly began the Spanish Enlightenment. In a vivid fashion they emphasize the polemical nature of this century that so loved to argue with itself.

So often this argumentative nature was counterproductive, but in this case looking back from the vantage of over two hundred years we can thank this peculiar nature for providing a wealth of greatly needed information. Finally, the polemics indicate how profoundly Feijoo's ideas had begun to stir up a general interest from the first day of their public appearance in 1726.

In order to know a bit more precisely what Feijoo had to say we shall look at several of his essays and letters. Their subject matter is diverse, and this very diversity in its totality demonstrates the newness and inventiveness of his ideas. The complete title of the first volume of the *Universal Theater* succinctly states the purpose behind it and all the volumes that were to follow: *Universal Theater of Criticism or Various Discourses Concerning All Kinds of Matters for the Unmasking of Common Errors.* Particularly illustrative is the beginning of the thirteenth discourse of volume three entitled: ''Philosophical Skepticism'':

There is so much latitude in the term skepticism and its degrees are so different that with this term, according to the wide extension given to its meaning, the most confusing error and the sanest method of philosophizing are both designated. In its rigid meaning skepticism is an extravagant delirium, in a more moderate one a prudent cautiousness. But those who in this century took the trouble to decry the most moderate skeptics, I know not whether from incomprehension or malice, confuse both meanings. Incomprehension in this matter is so blatant that I am persuaded that the problem arises rather from malice; and then malice is so detestable that I am persuaded it must be from lack of comprehension.

Although the Greek word *scepsis* ... means inquisitiveness, investigation, speculation, etc., usage has somewhat altered the meaning of this word so that today *skeptical* means doubting and *skepticism* that particular profession in which skeptics doubt and withhold their assent in controversial or debatable matters.

This doubt or suspension of agreement can be more or less rational according to the amount of treatment given a matter and according to the matter itself that is treated. Thus, while to doubt many things can be prudent, to doubt everything is insane.[3]

In addition to the validity of Feijoo's ideas expounded in this quotation the reader can appreciate the directness and simplicity of their expression, qualities that made Feijoo eminently readable to the public. The characteristic equanimity and fairness of his attitude is notable here too and helps to explain much of the reason for the public's interest and sympathy for his work. That Feijoo could lead his readers so gently into a matter that might have shaken their belief in certain political and religious dogmas illustrates his capacity for educating the public. His professorial prodding was of course at the core of this writing and is once again a prime reason for his ideas' success in provoking a response, often but not always favorable.

The very first discourse in the *Theater* is the well-known "Voz del pueblo" ("Voice of the People"). I quote from its beginning paragraphs to illustrate further Feijoo's determination to attack blind stupidity, so much his theme in the quotation above. We should not be alarmed at his seemingly "undemocratic" attitude. He is in effect condemning a mass mentality. The reference to the "masses" is therefore not significant:

That poorly understood maxim in which God supposedly speaks through the voice of the people authorized the masses to tyrannize good judgment and established in that voice a power capable of oppressing literary nobility. This is an error from which infinitely more errors are born because, once it is concluded that the masses express the truth, all their mistakes are venerated as divine inspirations. . . .

To distrust completely the popular voice one has only to reflect on the extravagant errors that have been and are committed in the names of religion, politics, and customs. Cicero said that there is no piece of foolishness so absurd that some philosopher has not somewhere affirmed it. With even more reason I say that there is no piece of foolishness so monstrous that it is not supported by the uniform consent of some people.

Whatever the light of natural reason represents as abominable in some place passed and still passes as licit. Lying, perjury, adultery, homicide, robbery — in short all the vices achieved or now achieve the general approbation of some nations. Among the old Germans robbery used to make the robber the owner of all he stole. Even more barbarous were the Caspians, people of Scythia, who imprisoned and caused to die from hunger their own parents when they reached an advanced age. . . . Everyone knows that in many parts of the Orient there is the barbaric custom of burning the wives alive when their husbands die. What can I say of the license that stupidity has in some nations? In Malabar the women can marry whatever husbands they want. On the island of Ceylon when a woman marries, she is the common property of all the brothers of the husband and the married couple can get a divorce whenever it wants in order to contract a new alliance.[4]

These last lines may have an amusing ring for some twentieth-century readers, yet they do underline Feijoo's basic intention —

that of revealing the folly of the "people's" wisdom. He is not criticizing one particular people or class but a pernicious attitude held by different groups and individuals in many parts of the world. These lines, then, illustrate Feijoo's underlying hatred of superstition, bigotry, and just plain ignorance.

In a fascinating essay entitled "Españoles americanos" ("Spanish Americans") (discourse 6 in volume 4) Feijoo strives, among other things, to argue away some prejudices that exist toward the *criollos*. This attitude especially in the early part of the eighteenth century is valuable in itself. What interests us, however, are some reflective lines midway through the discourse. Essentially, Feijoo continues his attack on the stupidity and blindness of the mass mind seen in the previous quotations:

It is not a question of the lack of a general enlightenment brilliant enough to undeceive man of a thousand old errors; it is rather a lack of reflection on man's part simply to make use of it. I do not know what mists they are that cloud the eyes of understanding so that man does not see, no matter how obvious it may be, the way to undeceive himself. There is no doubt that at times . . . it is merely a lack of the means to understand the truth. But experience has shown me that in most men there reigns an evil intellectual disposition by means of which common opinion is like a masking veil for them which hides the most evident truths. What is worse is that this evil intellectual disposition is found in men who otherwise are discreet and intelligent.[5]

Feijoo's essays take on a note of open indoctrination at times. It is then that we can see him at his professorial best, gently but severely urging a change in our behavior. This particular characteristic of his writing is seen in the tenth discourse of volume seven, entitled "Verdadera y falsa urbanidad" ("True and False Urbanity"). It is an excellent example of his procedure and style wherein he first establishes his theme, defines it in the most precise of terms, and then elaborates on it with all manner of details. This sort of presentation allows him to inject personal opinions, overlaid with a bit of honest didacticism. The whole effect is one of charming instruction. I quote from a subdivision concerning loquacity:

Great talkers are the laziest tyrants. In my opinion, which concedes a certain limited amount of reasoning to animals, the art of conversing is a gift even more personal than that of discoursing. He who always wants to be heard and not listen to anyone usurps from the others a special prerogative of their being. What does he achieve from his torrent of words? Nothing more than annoying his listeners who then undercut what he said, speaking disparagingly of him. No more time is wasted than that consumed in listening to great talkers. These are people who lack reflection. If they had it, they would be quiet in order not to be contemptible. If they lack reflection, then they also lack judgment. And he who lacks judgment, how can he ever talk with ability? And what good results are there for the listeners to a fool, except for the excercising of their patience? ... The fluxes of the tongue are so many opinionated vomitings of the soul: eruptions of a weak spirit that spews forth, before digesting it, the information it receives.[6]

This rather outspoken logic is found everywhere in Feijoo's writings. Another example somewhat less blunt is in one of his *Letters* (volume 4, number 25). The title is "May the author be excused from attempting to form a system of electricity." In general it deals with his preference for staying out of a field that publicly has elicited much formal study and much informal speculation. His ideas are forthright and at times are critical of certain theories that he chooses to comment on. As usual there are sufficient examples to illustrate his points. One of these concerns a young man whom he knows who was near a spot where lightning struck. He was not harmed other than from that moment he began to lose his hair, and in a few days had none at all. Feijoo asserts that there are several deductions that could be made from this incident, but he prefers one which he then expounds upon. The important thing here is not so much what he says but how he says it. His very ordered, logical mind proceeds steadily along, instructing us in the most useful way and at the same time "diverting" us with its reasonable cleverness. An excellent example of this Horatian method occurs earlier in the same letter where he discusses the variety of theories on electricity:

I, in truth, have read in the authors quoted as well as in others of the many experiments that have been made in various places up until now. But, Dear Sir, those experiments that are merely related are not of much use. It is necessary to see and "touch" them. Experience, in order to enlighten, must be one's own and not someone else's. Such a matter cannot be resolved by two different subjects, one who experiences it and another who discourses about it. Both must do the same thing, that is, experience it. I say this for several reasons. The first is that men not only discourse differently but they also see and look at things differently. And this, which may seem paradoxical, for me is a very evident truth. On what, except this diversity in *seeing* or *looking,* does what we experience at each step depend? For among those who see the same object ... their own concepts of what they saw are quite diverse. And then we must add to this the prolonged disputes about whether something is large or small or of such and such a shape or color, etc.[7]

One of his most touching and revealing letters is number 17 in volume 5 entitled "On the occasion of the author's explaining his conduct in his old age...." There are many statements here about the way he lives and feels, although the letter's purpose is to present some of his ideas about old age and how one achieves a certain stability and contentment in it. Below are some of his moving sentences:

It is true that I do not possess a brusque, angry personality, such a common disease among old people, whose lack I attribute in my own case in part to temperament and in part to reflection. I always remember that when I was a boy, I noted this attitude in the old, observing that this attitude infected all those about them. I thus try to avoid it. Above all I avoid censuring everything in the present, a propensity so often of the aged. Who would believe them would find that the world in the short space of forty or fifty years suffered a notable decadence in its customs. But can that really be so? Hardly. I have lived many years, and in the distance from my youth to my old age I not only did not observe that moral corruption, but rather it seems to me that the world is somewhat less bad today than it was fifty or sixty years ago....

These things that I have mentioned, wherein old people make themselves unpleasant to those they meet, cause considerable trouble or they prevent a great good — that is, the usefulness that their advice could provide to the young. If the young consider the old as rigid, stubborn censors, it is hardly to be expected that they will listen docilely to their instruction. What is worse, they may come to dismiss them mentally as impertinent and ridiculous. I think that it would not be very difficult for an older person to observe the rules that I practice in order not to be obnoxious to those with whom he lives and converses.[8]

Feijoo was a man who not only could teach people but who could understand them very well. This characteristic of his personality is of course the basic reason for his success with his large audience. He came across to his friends and his readers as someone intelligent and compassionate. As a literary artist Feijoo is not too important to us. This does not mean that he could not have been a novelist, because in his writing he is much like a journalist or a *costumbrista* writer, a keen and observant narrator of the contemporary scene. His renovation of ideas is his greatest contribution to eighteenth-century Spain. He is first and foremost a teacher who brought the Enlightenment to his students, the Spanish people. Because of him Oviedo became a sort of funnel through which new concepts flowed into the rest of the country. Feijoo's introduction of new ideas in philosphy and science is the real basis of his importance, therefore. The leadership that he gave to the nearly foundering beginning of the Spanish Enlightenment is his enormous contribution to Spanish culture. When we look at his French counterparts — who were several in number and somewhat later in time — we can only marvel all the more at this wise and kind gentleman.

II   *A Disciple of Feijoo*

There were of course other men important in the eighteenth-century awakening of Spain, although no "school" was formed such as that of the *Philosophes* in France. There were many supporters and defenders of Feijoo, as we have seen. We can take a brief look at one disciple, however, to see better what type of people these were and the sort of work that was done. This man in himself is very interesting principally because of his selfless dedication to investigative work and because he avoided popular recognition in most all forms.

Fray Martín Sarmiento was born in Galicia in 1695. At age fifteen he became a Benedictine and, almost literally, spent the rest of his life in the Convento de San Martín in Madrid where he died in 1771. He was one of the most productive writers Spain has ever produced. Yet because his work has remained unpublished, he is rarely recognized. It is quite ironic that the reputation of this man who perhaps did more than anyone to spread the fame of his mentor Feijoo has been eclipsed by others of the time. Sarmiento's oblivion cannot be blamed totally on others, nevertheless. During his lifetime he refused to let his research be published, except on a most unusual occasion, as when he publicly defended Feijoo in his *Demostración apologética* (*Apologetic Demonstration,* 1732). Possessed of a sensitive, hermetic personality he refused to allow the public to tear apart his work in the ceaseless polemics that were so much a part of the times. The attacks that he received from his defense of Feijoo may have been a major reason for his refusal. At any rate, what we do find in Sarmiento's case is an enormous amount of research on a wide variety of subjects, particularly literary, linguistic, and scientific. Most of his manuscripts lie in repositories in Madrid. Some have been copied and are spread about. For example, a copy of his important document on Cervantes' birthplace is in The Hispanic Society of America. Copies of Sarmiento's works, as well as some manuscripts themselves, have become dispersed in great part because he sent them to friends who wrote asking questions of one kind or another.

His "Noticia de la verdadera patria (Alcalá) de El Miguel de Cervantes" ("Notice of the True Birthplace [Alcalá] of Miguel de Cervantes") has value for various reasons. In the early 1700s Cervantes' birthplace was unknown. The first person to discover anything concrete was Juan de Iriarte, who found in the Royal Library a reference to it in a list of captives in northern Africa. Iriarte sent this information to his good friend Sarmiento, who related what he himself discovered to his friends. It was left to them to publish the material. Since they did not, it is little known that Sarmiento wrote the above-mentioned manuscript in which he discusses the importance of his findings. He definitely locates the until-then generally unknown birthplace, in a most succinct and subdued manner, thus contributing much to Cervantean investigations in the eighteenth century. His very serious addition to the development of these investigations comes at a time when Cervantes and his work were still not taken too seriously. Because Sarmiento's discoveries have lain dormant so long they astonish us with their hitherto unrecognized novelty.[9]

After Sarmiento's death his study of Spanish poetry and poets was published. Written in 1745 it was printed in 1775 as the intended first volume of a series that was never continued. The book is entitled *Memorias para la historia de la poesía española y poetas españoles* (*Notes on the History of Spanish Poetry and Poets*). It is a very important volume that can be interpreted as the first analytical attempt at studying Spanish poetry as a whole, showing origins, early directions, and apexes throughout the medieval period. There are several discoveries in it of much singularity and vision. The most significant concerns the epic poem about the Cid. Truly scientific investigation of this literary masterpiece was then in its infancy. It would be some thirty years after this that Tomás Antonio Sánchez would publish his important volumes. When speaking of ballads as a genre Sarmiento correctly identifies the earliest extant copy of the *Poema del mío Cid*.[10]

III *Intellectualism*

So often the Spanish eighteenth century has been accused of being dry and empty of thought. What this criticism has failed to see is the richness in the intellectual endeavors it rather foolishly decries as sterile. It is in this period that the foundations are laid for the modern scientific investigation of literature. In this section we shall look at two writers, both of them outstanding examples of this early intellectualism. And in the next section we shall see investigative endeavors applied in one specific direction — toward the "discovery" of Cervantes.

Juan de Iriarte was born in 1702 in the Canary Islands. At a very early age he was sent to Paris for his education, and later in other parts of France his avid interest in letters began to mature. At the Collège de Louis-le-Grand (where Voltaire was also a pupil) he studied principally languages, philosophy, and mathematics. It was here too that he read and studied the writers of antiquity who became mentors for the remainder of his life in Madrid, where he moved in 1724.

Evidently Iriarte originally intended to follow a career in law, but he became so interested in the holdings of the Royal Library that he never really made a serious attempt to disregard his call to the field of letters. Receiving the attention first of the head librarian and then of the dukes of Béjar and Alba, by 1732 he had become an official member of the library staff. This position was doubly important to him, for, in addition to allowing him to live with financial security, it gave him more time for his favorite pursuits: criticism, philology, and bibliography. Juan de Friarte soon became an outstanding literary critic. When the *Diary of the Writers of Spain* first appeared, he became a frequent contributor. His first article in this journal was a review of Jacinto Segura's *Norte crítico, con las reglas más ciertas para la discreción en la historia (Critical Guide, Containing the Most Certain Rules for Discretion in History),* which had been printed in 1733. Segura was one of Feijoo's harshest critics, and Friarte in his review takes Segura to task for what he considers very unfair criticism. Ultimately Juan de Friarte found himself immersed in the polemic between the pro- and anti-Feijoo camps.

In 1747 he became a member of the Royal Academy of the Language, where he continued his participation in the composing and editing of the academy's *Grammar* and *Dictionary.* As curator of manuscripts in the Royal Library he compiled a careful and complete index, gathered material for his *Bibliotheca Graeca* (*Greek Library*), composed an essay on *Paleografía griega* (*Greek Paleography*), and worked as well on other no less worthy endeavors. He wrote a great deal of poetry in Latin, and this seems to have been a kind of relaxation for him. Being quick of mind, he was an excellent composer of epigrams. He wrote some seven hundred of his own, translated more than one hundred by other composers into Latin, and rendered more than two hundred of Martial's into Spanish. In 1754 he was made director of a project to produce a Latin-Spanish dictionary, but in 1758, due to illness and overwork, he was forced to withdraw from this task. Unfortunately the dictionary was never compiled.

At the same time that he was laboring on these projects he was working on his *Gramática latina, escrita con nuevo método y nuevas observaciones, en verso castellano, con su explicación en prosa* (*Latin Grammar, Written With a New Method and New Observations, in Spanish Verse, With Explanations in Prose*), which he never saw published, although it was at the printer's when he died in 1771. His nephews collected and published his remaining works. This endeavor was made possible through the generosity of certain nobles and the Princes Gabriel, Luis, and Antonio. Such a generous act indirectly shows the intimate ties that Juan de Iriarte enjoyed with members of the royal court.

In a letter to Juan de Iriarte's nephew Bernardo, Father Enrique Flórez, confessor and friend of the former, gives a good résumé of what and who Juan de Iriarte was:

But I especially recall that rare combination of talents which he possessed, that universal knowledge of everything in particular, that very delicate taste that intuited the finest in everything, that great humility toward everything he knew, that mouth whose lips never maligned anyone . . . that pure and fragile conscience that put God first and that always both edified and confused me. The suffering, patience, and resignation that he demonstrated in his last days in the continuous afflictions with which the Lord purified him moved me many times, seeing a man of such irreproachable character beg me to ask God to forgive him.[11]

Juan de Iriarte's greatest contribution to eighteenth-century letters has often been considered his education of Tomás, his nephew. While this is indeed true and in itself gives us a very good idea as to the educational upbringing of the most outstanding *Ilus-*

trados, it tends to deny him the rightful admiration he deserves as one of those prolific, indefatigable investigators such as Sarmiento and Sánchez. It is to men like Iriarte that we owe a tremendous debt for their extraordinary labors in private and public libraries ferreting out many facts that we today accept unthinkingly but that in the 1700s were not generally known.

Tomás Antonio Sánchez was born in 1725. Like so many literary investigators of this century he pursued a career in the church. He left this eventually to become librarian of the Royal Library where he worked on the *Bibliotheca Hispana Nova* (*New Spanish Library*) of the seventeenth-century erudite Nicolás Antonio. He became a member of several learned societies, principal among which was the Royal Academy of the Language. He died in 1802 in Madrid.[12]

Whenever the *Poema de mío Cid* is mentioned today, Sánchez' name is prominent, for it was he who in 1779 published the first modern edition of this ancient national epic. The first of four volumes (1779–1790) included the poem and also a study of the marquis of Santillana. This writer and his work were the subject of investigations by men such as Sarmiento as well. Santillana's own interest in earlier and contemporary authors elicited much attention from these eighteenth-century compilers of detail who saw in those previous works foundations for their own revolutionary pursuits. The second volume of Sánchez' series contained the works of Alonso de Berceo, Spain's earliest lyric poet. The third was a publication of the *Libro de Aleixandre* (*Book of Alexander*). The fourth was a publication of the work of the archpriest of Hita, Juan Ruiz. A fifth volume was prepared containing Pero López de Ayala's *Rimado de Palacio* (*Palace Rhyme Book*), the last important example of the poetic strophe called *cuaderna vía*. It was not printed for lack of the necessary subscribers.

As we have already indicated, Sánchez' real importance lies in his publishing Spain's greatest epic for the first time. We still often, and mistakenly, identify the interest in national literature, especially the medieval, with the romantic outburst of the 1830s. Sánchez' publication disproves such claims quite decisively, and, to repeat, it is really in the eighteenth century that a vibrant interest in national literary themes occurs. Not only was the Sánchez publication important in Spain but in the rest of Europe as well, for Sánchez was actually the first editor of any European epic. We might recall at this point that the French *Chanson de Roland* (*Song of Roland*) was not published until 1837. The earlier Spanish date thus takes on an added meaning for Spanish culture. And there is another reason to praise Sánchez' work — in his commentary on the poem he points out those qualities that we have come to accept as natural and inherent in it. Sánchez is the first to emphasize that the *Poema de mío Cid* is a valuable outpouring of the people's sensibilities as witnessed in its essentially simple and popular tones.

From the standpoint of the twentieth century, now that the procedure for the scientific investigation of literary works has been established for years — and due much to the efforts of Sánchez and others like him — it is easy to find fault with some of the editing in the four volumes of his publication. But such faultfinding is unfair when we consider that no one had done this sort of thing before. The fact that for the first time an epic poem of great national and historical import is published in any European country gives Spaniards and those concerned with Spanish literature great pride. The additional fact that such publishing was done, for the most part, with accurate editing is more reason for praise. Editorial faults, especially in Juan Ruiz' *Libro de buen amor* (*Book of Good Love*) which exhibits errors that are embarrassing today, are certainly there, but to dwell on these is to ignore Sánchez' trailblazing effort. It is also to forget the faulty texts themselves that he had to work with. The archpriest's *Book* still presents scholars with very difficult problems. That they existed in the eighteenth century in the infancy of true literary investigation is not at all surprising and should be understood by those who continue to criticize the mistakes in these innovative eighteenth-century editions.

In the midst of all his erudite productivity Sánchez somehow found time to tangle with that indefatigable polemicist, Forner. We will not go into the details of their quarrel except to note Forner's *Carta de Bartolo* (1790) which evidences rather clearly his inability to understand what his own century was really all about. Essentially he attacked Sánchez in his most salient attribute, that of preserver of the national literature. Forner saw in the editor of these ''old'' manuscripts simply a commentator on useless antiquities. What is startlingly ironic is Forner's designation of the poem on the Cid itself as a piece of propaganda about an exaggeratedly important feudal chieftain. This revelatory piece of criticism from Forner nicely delineates his own shortcomings as a critic, which we have seen already, and underscores the solidity of Sánchez' bold, visionary publications.

IV   *Cervantean Investigations*

As a further example of the erudition and basic investigatory impulses of the eighteenth century, we look at another aspect of the Spanish prose of the period. The eighteenth century is often combined with the seventeenth century in the latter's failure to understand the underlying meaning of *Don Quixote*. Yet it is during the 1700s that the first serious investigations of both Cervantes and his *Don Quixote* occur. Whereas the more romantic, idealistic interpretations of the knight-errant's exploits must await the next century, it was during the eighteenth century that the solid bases of Cervantean investigations were laid. The discoveries about Cervantes' life, the beginning of a modern comprehension of his two great characters, and the elevation of both Cervantes and *Don Quixote* to classical pedestals, all are developments of the eighteenth century. In the next few pages we shall look at the most outstanding of the scholars who were responsible for these developments. Ironically they still are not nearly so well known as their achievements demand.

Gregorio Mayans y Siscar was a Valencian, a contemporary of Feijoo, though somewhat more outspoken in his ideas and procedures. At odds with several other scholars during his lifetime, he established a name for himself with his *Vida de Cervantes* (*Life of Cervantes*, 1737), luxuriously published in Lord Carteret's London edition of *Don Quixote*. This was really the first genuine biography of Cervantes and as such has great value. Of even more significance are some of the concepts in the work. To understand these we must look for a moment at the evaluation of Cervantes and Alonso Fernández de Avellaneda in the early eighteenth century.

It is very hard to imagine that at one time Avellaneda's *Don Quixote* was considered more important than that of Cervantes. Since its publication in 1614 Avellaneda's work had not received much attention. With its translation into French in 1704 some scholars came to judge it superior to Cervantes' work, however. In 1732 a new edition in Spanish appeared under the aegis of two important critics of the moment, Blas Antonio Nasarre and Agustín de Montiano y Luyando. Montiano especially lauded Avellaneda as the better author. As in the French translation, the reasons for this high praise derived from the supposed "symmetry" to be found more in evidence in Avellaneda's *Don Quixote*.

In 1736 while hard at work on his *Life of Cervantes* Mayans vividly recalls Montiano's frank statements and proceeds to write his own work in direct refutation of the former's ideas. With his essay we thus have the public appearance of another of those bitter, almost interminable literary polemics. Mayans repudiates the most salient points made by Montiano and his group. In other words, he attacks a whole school of thought that would give only the slightest value to Cervantes' genius, a genius whose acceptance in the first part of the century was precarious at best. Throughout his work, understanding his own intentions very well, Mayans repeatedly lauds Cervantes' originality and genius, affirming, in direct contrast to Montiano, his superior qualities as a writer and interpreter of the human condition.

Mayans' essay is the first significant study of Cervantes. That it comes in the early 1700s inspires once again the recollection of the significant fact that it is the eighteenth century that starts and develops serious investigations of Cervantes and *Don Quixote*. While the public in general might find only amusing scenes in the novel, a few scholars were becoming increasingly aware of the book's philosophical import. Mayans' *Life* is not a grand biography of the sort we would expect today. Yet its very innovativeness of attitude and energetic defense of its subject show us that by the 1730s Cervantes and his novel could no longer be dismissed as tasteless, raucous, or asymmetrical. Mayans understood well the aesthetics of the work and the genius of its author. He also had the necessary determination to defend them and ultimately to propel them into the consciousness of his own and succeeding generations.

As we noted earlier in the present chapter Martín Sarmiento also contributed to the advancement of Cervantean criticism in the 1700s. His unpublished piece is quite important because for the first time Cervantes' birthplace, Alcalá de Henares, is definitely established. Mayans himself had said it was Madrid.[13] In one of the many interesting comments in his manuscript Sarmiento emphasizes the tremendous need for a commentary on *Don Quixote*. This greatest contribution of the *Ilustrados* to Cervantean criticism is actually the work of an Englishman, the Reverend John Bowle of Idmiston near Salisbury, who provided a commentary and index when he published his unique edition of *Don Quixote* in 1781. This is the first annotated edition of the novel, and with its appearance we may say that modern Cervantean criticism as we know it today actually begins. John Bowle (1725–1788) was one of those English parsons who in the eighteenth century so loved to involve themselves in literary and antiquarian investigations. There was nothing necessarily distinguishing about Bowle's personality except for his tenacity and forthrightness. These characteristics more often than not caused him needless difficulties. They also provided him with the ability to engage in protracted research that, lamentably, gave him little recognition in his own day and that only now, some two hundred years later, is deservedly esteemed for its intrinsic worth.

Bowle's interests first were directed toward antiquarian pursuits and, partly as a result, English literature. This fascination with anything old — houses, monumental inscriptions, towns, genealogy, languages — was widespread. There were several antiquarian societies, the most prestigious being the Society of Antiquaries of London to which Bowle was elected in 1767. At age forty-two he thus achieved a certain renown that brought him to the attention of many notable figures of his day. Among these were the Warton brothers and Horace Walpole. From his involvement in English antiquities and literature came his defense of Milton against the libelous charges of William Lauder.[14] Bowle's long essay, *A True State of the Controversy Concerning Milton,* written in 1750, was the first discovery of Lauder's forgeries and misrepresentations. Unfortunately, it has never been published. John Douglas, who was actually the first to print a vindication of Milton, did note Bowle as being the first real discoverer, while later critics have for the most part overlooked his contributions.

From English Bowle progressed to the study of foreign languages and literatures. He took up French initially but soon became more interested in Italian literature, notably the epic romance of the sixteenth century. He possessed a great facility for languages and quickly learned their grammatical idiosyncracies. This ability, especially evident in his rapid acquisition of written Spanish, was noted in later years by Dr. Thomas Percy, who went so far as to suggest that Bowle knew more about Spanish literature than anyone of his day. This was high praise indeed and seems all the more significant when we realize that Bowle never traveled to Spain nor was able to speak Spanish with any fluency. He was entirely a self-taught man therefore but one who instructed himself so well that he composed — in Spanish — the first modern edition of *Don Quixote.*

Bowle's deep interest in languages and literatures presents a further fascinating aspect of his career that in a way makes him even more singular. Because of his scholarly pursuits he was a man much caught up in the intellectual life of his day. He was also an individ-

ual who personifies well the beloved Horatian *beatus ille.* Bowle
was content to lead the quiet life of a country parson and gentleman farmer. In much of his private correspondence he relates his
joy in hunting, planting, and harvesting. The call and attraction of
the land that repeatedly appear in these communications portray
someone who was well aware of the beauties of nature but who also
knew natures's ugliness and occasional crudities. This close relation
to the earth thus paradoxically created in Bowle both a naive idealism and much common sense.

There would appear some correlation in the attitudes of Sarmiento and Bowle. But while the former preferred to retreat into
his work and enjoy it only with himself and his friends, Bowle utilized the knowledge he received from other than purely erudite
sources. This fact makes him, for us, more human. It enabled him
to push the publication of his works, with one exception, and ultimately to become involved in rather violent polemics. In this sense
he was not unlike Mayans.

Bowle's ability to tackle grand projects like his edition of *Don
Quixote* is a good example of his idealism and inherent judicious-
ness. Without his vision of enthroning Cervantes among the classic
greats of literature he never would have started his work, much less
carried it to completion. And without his realistic, bulldog determination to have it well received among his peers as its, and his
own, due, the work might never have been published. The lack of
public acceptance and eventual attack by two vociferous enemies
notably elicited his bluntness and ironic sense of life. Unfortunately
these latter qualities were not enough to deter his opponents — nor
his death in 1788 as an almost certain result of their polemics.

With the 1781 edition of *Don Quixote,* Bowle makes us realize
that by the last half of the eighteenth century Cervantes' novel has
reached a point where it needs explaining. He is the first person to
do something about it. In his edition we are confronted with two
attitudes: the need to clarify what is sometimes no longer immediately comprehensible and the desire to establish *Don Quixote*
definitively as a classical work. The extraordinary thing is that only
Bowle carries out this enormous project. He finds much encouragement in Sarmiento's words to which we have previously referred.
(He had a copy of Sarmiento's manuscript in his library.) It is as if
the other studies we have noted were leading up to this one. Bowle
too seems to have sensed this in a way, especially in his high regard
for Sarmiento and his frequent quoting of him in his letters and in

several places in the *Anotaciones* of his edition.

One of the principal points of attack on Bowle was the need itself for a commentary. He was bitterly criticized for being so presumptuous, so said one enemy, as to think the novel needed explaining or that he might have intelligence enough to explain it. As we have seen, Bowle was not the only one to see the necessity for notes such as his. It is to Bowle's credit then that he persevered in his labors, for some thirteen years poring over endless books of chivalry, Italian epics, and medieval and Golden-Age poetry in order to carry out his grandiose project. There were indeed many passages in *Don Quixote* that were no longer readily clear. There were numerous place names and references to persons that meant nothing to many readers. Bowle's realization that the novel must have clarification and his determination to remedy the problem are basically why we should honor him. His more visionary dream of enthroning *Don Quixote* among the literary classics is a laudable material result. Even though by the last quarter of the century there were statements by various critics proclaiming Cervantes an author on the level of Dante and others, it is essentially because of Bowle's efforts alone that Cervantes and his novel achieve that very status.

There are others who worked with the *Quixote* in this period. Most notable are Vicente de los Rios, whose biography of Cervantes appeared in the academy's fine edition of the novel in 1780, and Juan Antonio Pellicer. His own edition at the end of the century included much annotation based on Bowle's earlier findings. Unfortunately, not only did he usually fail to note his sources but, incredibly, attacked Bowle at every turn. This pattern of behavior appeared in later critics as well. As a result Bowle's discoveries were not valued for their intrinsic worth until our own time.

It is to Mayans, Sarmiento, and Bowle that we are therefore greatly indebted. The two Spaniards considered Cervantes a serious writer of purpose and genius. This was particularly seen in Mayans' case when he forcefully defended him against the pro-Avellaneda forces. Bowle obviously defended him as well. While establishing Cervantes as a classical author and *Don Quixote* as a classic work, he proclaims that essentially eighteenth-century interpretation of the novel that probably originated with John Locke. That is, Don Quixote is not the messiah the later romantics and Unamuno will make of him. Cervantes through Don Quixote is condemning principally man's lack of equilibrium and proper judgment. Don Quixote really is a buffoon as the more supercilious viewpoint of the seventeenth and eighteenth centuries maintained. But Bowle sees in the sad figure of the knight a moral lesson for us all. This interpretation repeatedly appears in his private letters dealing with his work on the 1781 edition and represents the very serious attitude toward Cervantes in this century. Bowle's tremendous achievement is all the more outstanding when we realize how thorough a knowledge he had to have of another country's language and customs before he could attempt to produce a work like his.

V *Aesthetics*

We recall from above that the Jesuits were expelled from Spain in 1767 for predominantly political reasons. Among these exiles was the most outstanding of eighteenth-century Spanish aestheticians, Esteban de Arteaga. While his work was produced mainly outside Spain, he is still one of the most important Spanish literary voices of his time.

Of Basque origin Arteaga was born in 1747 in Segovia. He became a Jesuit in Madrid and indeed his youth was about the only part of his life spent in Spain. Like many other unfortunate Jesuits forced to leave precipitately he made his way eventually to Corsica. He left the Jesuits in a couple of years in hopes of being allowed to return home. His hopes were never realized, and he spent the remainder of his life in exile. Between 1773 and 1778 he studied at the University of Bologna. It was here that he became truly interested in the acquisition of encyclopedic knowledge. It is to this period that we are indebted particularly for the origins of his research and eventual published work. His interest in music and acquaintance with contemporary composers were similar outgrowths of this period. *Le rivoluzioni del teatro musicale italiano (Revolutions in the Italian Musical Theater)* was published between 1783 and 1785. Like his later works it is erudite, offering both facts and commentary concerning the theater in Italy. Like virtually any work of criticism in this century, the *Revolutions* elicited much comment and discussion. Some of Arteaga's more acerbic statements provoked attacks, unusually severe, and polemics ensued. This pattern of commentary and polemics would plague Arteaga until the end of his life.

In 1786 he came under the protection of an Aragonese diplomat, José Nicolás de Azara, and went to Rome to be nearer the source of this new aid. It was here that he wrote his most important work that established his reputation as Spain's foremost aesthetician. *La belleza ideal (Ideal Beauty)* was published in Madrid in 1789. Its much longer title is *Investigaciones filosóficas sobre la belleza ideal considerada como objeto de todas las artes de imitacion (Philosophical Investigations Concerning Ideal Beauty Considered as an Object of All the Arts of Imitation).* As this longer title implies, the work is complicated and complex in its ideas. Essentially these concern imitation in the process of artistic creation. According to one recent author,[15] Arteaga goes beyond early neoclassical tenets and evidences decidedly romantic tendencies in his discussion. Arteaga's focus is on man and his emotions as he maintains that the power of the artist's reason is diminished by his feelings and tastes. He asserts that the ugly aspects as well as the beauties of nature must be imitated. His greatest emphasis is on a different interpretation of "imitation." He means not merely a copy of nature but a creation of something new. Art is thus more than just "imitación servil"; it becomes Arteaga's "imitación ideal." He means by this that the more extensive and exemplary the artist's expression of the human experience in his work the more valid is his artistic statement.

In many ways Arteaga's views here and elsewhere are a synthesis of the evolving theory of aesthetics in the eighteenth century. In this evolution Arteaga's ideas at times may seem quite futuristic. His relative lack of interest in the cold, more formal aspect of the work of art and his emphasis on fantasy and passion in artistic creation do appear to announce the more liberal, intimate attitude of the later romantic philosophy. Whatever our interpretation today of him and his work we must see him as Spain's preeminent interpreter of artistic theory in the second half of the eighteenth century. Because of his exile and resultant cosmopolitanism he can be further appreciated for his contributions to the advancement of European intellectual endeavor in this period.

VI *Travel*

During the eighteenth century there existed an extraordinary vogue for traveling. In fact, it is actually during this time that the concept of touring originates. Whether the tourists were going to another county — "Abroad" as the English came to say — or simply to another section of their own country they became excellent observers of the scene about them. As a result some of the best literary productions, often forgotten or simply overlooked today, are a result of the travels of both literary artists and ordinary people out to enjoy a change of scenery. In this section we shall consider four representatives. Each is quite different; yet they nicely demonstrate what this sort of writing involved.

Of the four, Antonio Ponz is perhaps most significant as a "travel" writer. His *Viaje de España (Travels Through Spain)* is a voluminous study of Spanish places, objects, and monuments. Ponz was born in 1725 in Valencia. As with so many literary figures of the time he started out on a religious career but left his studies at age twenty-one to go to Madrid. Here he became involved in more mundane studies and eventually went to Italy where his fascination with art and antiquities became complete. Returning to Spain about the time of the expulsion of the Jesuits, he was given the task, for him a pleasant one, of inventorying the vast art collections they left behind.[16]

From this enterprise he became more and more fascinated with the idea of traveling around the Spanish countryside inventorying national works of art, as it were. His informative *Travels* came about from this rather simple beginning. The undertaking began about 1770 and the first volume of what would be many appeared in 1772. During the writing of his work Ponz received many accolades and honors as well as negative criticism, but the work stands as a monument to him and the investigative propensities of his time.

We should feel much indebted to the author, for the work is no ordinary travelogue or diary but a vast catalogue of works of art that unfortunately in some cases are now lost. Written with verve and straightforwardness, the eighteen volumes were published between 1772 and 1794, the last finished by a nephew after Ponz' death in 1792. Ponz' attitude toward what he describes is for the most part loving and appreciative. When we remember that medieval architecture was not often praised by the eighteenth century, his fair descriptions of medieval and baroque treasures are to be highly valued. It is not only descriptions of artistic treasures that he provides. Throughout the volumes is the insistent enlightened call to preserve and build. There is persistent urging to improve roads and bridges, to protect the land, and at the same time to increase industrial production. These calls are so inherently a part of the 1700s that it seems only appropriate that they should appear in a work whose purpose at first glance is to list relics of the past. As a final attraction the didacticism of the work is softened by its often conversational, natural style. Even when Ponz is vehemently preaching to us we are beguiled by the pleasant, even soothing, flow of his words. His *Travels,* today not well known, merits appreciation and can afford us many hours of relaxing reading.

Guillermo Bowles (1705–1780) — not to be confused with John Bowle — was a writer of an entirely different sort. Born William Bowles, he was a naturalist who went to Paris in 1740 to study and eventually ended up in Spain. Because of his background and partly due to political connections he was appointed superintendent of state mines. In this capacity he traveled throughout Spain investigating its minerals and natural history, living chiefly in Madrid and Bilbao. He died in Madrid. His best-known work, a direct outgrowth of his official position, was his *Introduction to the Natural History and Physical Geography of Spain* (1775). It generated much interest and controversy on its appearance. Quite the opposite of Ponz' voluminous study, this is a work dealing specifically with the Spain of Bowles' day. In England Bowles had a certain popularity as a result of his book. In fact, demand became such that in just a few years another writer published a similar work that was in great part based on Bowles' investigations.

Sir John Talbot Dillon (1740?–1805) was born in Ireland and was a member of the Irish parliament from 1776 to 1783. For much of this period he traveled about Europe. In 1780 he was made a baron of the Holy Roman Empire by the Emperor Joseph II in recognition of his services in parliament on behalf of his Roman Catholic fellow subjects. He was much interested in Spain and her literature and became at one time a close friend of John Bowle while the latter was at work on his edition of *Don Quixote.* Dillon's most noteworthy publication was his *Travels in Spain* (1780). It contains his own and William Bowles' observations on the natural history and geography of Spain. Through his reediting of much of Bowles' material, the latter's work became even more popular. Dillon wrote several other volumes, particularly on Spain. Perhaps most outstanding is the further manifestation of English interest — especially during a time when the English and Spanish were at war — in Spanish geography, culture, and literature.

Gaspar Melchor de Jovellanos represents for many Hispanists the epitome of the eighteenth-century enlightened Spaniard. This is not to say that his contemporaries did not possess the same characteristics and capacities that he did. Certainly we have already seen the extraordinary abilities of many others. Jovellanos, rather, had so many different interests — literary, political, educational, historical, and economic — that he very well personifies the ideal Spanish *Ilustrado*. Jovellanos did not always stand out in each of the fields he so energetically pursued, but when we look at the total picture of his endeavors we are immediately impressed by his accomplishments. The reader may think it a bit strange that I choose to discuss Jovellanos at this point, because ordinarily he is studied more from the political and economic point of view. In his last years Jovellanos, while a political exile, wrote some fascinating essays that fit very nicely into the present section of this book. Since they also present a very lyrical, sentimental side of Jovellanos, I think a discussion of him and these essays is called for here.

Jovellanos was born in Gijón on January 5, 1744. He studied at the Universities of Oviedo, Ávila, Osma, and Alcalá de Henares. In 1768, on completion of law studies, he was appointed a criminal magistrate in Seville. From that same year we can probably date his earliest known poems. In 1775 he joined the Economic Society of Seville, beginning his participation in these societies all over Spain. As an example, when he went to Madrid in 1778 as a civil magistrate, he joined the Economic Society there. In 1780 he was elected to the Academies of History and Fine Arts, and in 1781 he met, after several years of correspondence, a young man whom he greatly influenced in his formative years, Juan Meléndez Valdés. In 1782 he began a series of letters to Antonio Ponz describing landscapes, architecture, and customs. These letters were exchanged during a period of ten years and mark the beginning of his interest in antiquities and travel. Jovellanos was sent into a sort of semiexile in 1790 for trying to help his friend Francisco de Cabarrús, the founder of the first national bank in Spain who had recently fallen from grace. From this time on Jovellanos was in and out of favor in Madrid. On October 16, 1797, he was appointed ambassador to Russia, and then, almost incredibly, this appointment was superseded by his appointment as minister of justice on November 27. Less than a year later he lost this position and had to return to Asturias.

In 1800 secret accusations were leveled against him and on March 13, 1801, Jovellanos was arrested and soon confined in the Carthusian monastery of Valldemossa on Mallorca. On May 5, 1802, he was transferred to the castle of Bellver outside Palma. Between 1802 and 1807 he composed several studies concerning the castle and Palma. (It is these treatises that interest us now.) Ferdinand VII ordered Jovellanos released in 1808. Until his death in 1811 Jovellanos was once again in the midst of political upheaval.[17]

As we have noted, Jovellanos was involved in an enormous variety of endeavors of all sorts. Throughout his life he was concerned with the countryside of Spain, both from a conservationist and an artistic point of view. While he was on Mallorca this concern became especially evident. As Professor Polt notes, three factors caused this energetic concern: excessive leisure time, a need for distraction, and the desire to help the art historian Ceán Bermúdez, to whom he addressed these writings.[18]

The *Memoria del Castillo de Bellver, descripción histórico-artística* or *Descripción del castillo de Bellver (Essay on the Castle of Bellver: An Historical-Artistic Description* or *Description of the Castle of Bellver)* is a vivid discussion of the old castle outside Palma. As well, it is a sort of *costumbrista* rendering of the geology, flora, fauna, and festivals of the entire region. Jovellanos also conjures up scenes from the castle's past. In an appendix, *Memorias del Castillo de Bellver (Memoirs of the Castle of Bellver)*, we are given a history of the building from the fourteenth to the eighteenth centuries.

The *Descripción panorámica del Castillo de Bellver (A Panoramic Description of the Castle of Bellver)* is a sort of "photographic" guide to the landscape as seen from the tower of the castle. Two essays that are now appended to the *Description* really belong to the *Panoramic Description,* since they treat in much detail some buildings that can be seen at a distance.

Jovellanos wrote other essays while here on Mallorca but the ones just mentioned serve our purposes very well. Ponz was concerned with an extensive cataloging of Spain's antiquities, and Bowles and Dillon with enumerating her physical attributes. Jovellanos is concerned with this too, but his narration is imbued with a certain amount of feeling and sentiment that is not so evident in the others. This sentiment or even nostalgia that comes from the contemplation of the countryside and its monuments is significant in considering travel literature as a worthy literary effort. We may also see here further indication of a growing romanticism in literary production of the period, this from the pen of one who essentially retained his neoclassical orientation.

As an example of Jovellanos' writing we may look at the following passages:

From the platform of the just-mentioned bridge one passes to the tower of homage and inside it one goes up and down along a narrow passage which gives entrance to its rooms. There are five of these, all round.... There is nothing in them that does not indicate having been made more for a jail than for normal habitation. Very thick walls, doors with heavy locks and bars, high windows covered by narrow and thick iron grillwork, and other such defenses that greed has carried away but whose marks could not be erased all witness the rooms' sad fate. But this realization is heightened even more in the most interior room called the Well, and not unreasonably, since it seems more appropriate as a sepulcher for dead bodies than live ones.... One's spirit is horrified at this living tomb, and if on one hand he realizes that there is no crime which the perversity of man cannot reach, on the other hand he cannot help admiring the number of those who have aspired to excellence in the horrible art of tormenting their fellowman. It is fortunately somewhat distracting to reflect on other objects that this castle had in another time, since it is said that it was constructed as a palace for the kings of Mallorca.... Who, then, would not stop to contemplate it in those other days...? In another time and situation, what different scenes these rooms would present, today destroyed, solitary, and silent.[19]

Into this very clear, direct description the sentimental tone of the idealist nicely intrudes. In the last lines the theme of *ubi sunt* (where are they?) rises to the surface in an almost yearning and surely melancholy way. The ambience is much like that of Shelley's famous poem "Ozymandias." Behind the cold façade of a physical description there lies the incipient emotion of the romantic literary artist. Jovellanos' most serenely neoclassical writing often betrays this emotion. For us in this section of our chapter, however, this obvious sentiment underscores further the significance of Spanish eighteenth-century "travel" literature. It was a vogue popular and varied in form and theme, significantly indicative of new directions in literary philosophy.

VII   *Writers of Fiction: Torres Villarroel, Isla, Montengón, and Cadalso*

Of all the writers of the Spanish eighteenth century Diego de Torres Villarroel is perhaps the most titillating and elusive to us today. One has only to read recent critical works with their often divergent interpretations of his work to understand this statement. Torres hardly fits any mold of the century; that is, he is neither purely traditionalist nor *Ilustrado*. He was born in 1694 in Salamanca, the son of a bookseller. At the university of his native city he began his studies, but true to his erratic personality he became involved in other more fascinating occupations such as pamphleteer, bullfighter, soldier, dancing instructor, thief, etc. While some of these occupations were hardly edifying, they did provide him a very ample view of life which would serve him well in composing his works. In pursuing his "career" he traveled a great deal, coming to know many sorts of people and testing his quite masterful art of living. For some time he was under the protection of the countess of Arcos and the duchess of Alba. The attainment of this protection is an excellent example of his innate abilities at conning his fellowman. It must be said, however, that he did become more respectable as he matured and thus was able to mix among levels of society that his birth would otherwise have prevented. As early as 1726 he was appointed professor of mathematics at the University of Salamanca. This experience forms one of the most amusing — and satirical — in his *Vida* (*Life*), first published in 1742. There are other works of Torres, most notably his *Visiones y visitas de Torres con don Francisco de Quevedo por la corte* (*Visions and Visits of Torres and Francisco de Quevedo in Madrid*). Torres died in 1770.

In our presentation of Torres we shall consider him and those two works. Torres' *Life* is often considered an example of the picaresque novel. This label is not entirely correct. The work is really just as contradictory as its author, and in this way reflects its autobiographical character. Torres himself refers to it as both picaresque and not picaresque. Intentionally he has included something of the picaresque, adapting an existent form to new literary intentions. He wants to write the life of a contemporary man but one presented in a traditional literary format. To describe such a person as himself — bourgeois, self-made, charlatan, intellectual, sycophant — there was no really prescribed mode. Autobiographies usually came from great church or political figures, people well established who were certain of their place in life and affirmed it quite consciously. Torres, this man of many psychological conflicts, chose a style that paints both the good and the bad, a new twist in novelistic technique certainly and one that prefigures that of the psychological realistic novel of the late nineteenth century. He thus links that first great Spanish novelist, Cervantes, and the realists of the 1800s. We find in this autobiography the story of two distinct characters — both a knave and a saint.

The *Life* should be seen then as a daring new sort of autobiography with picaresque traits. Its title could just as well be something like the *History of an Ordinary Person* or the *Intimate Story of a Bourgeois*. This latter title would be most intriguing, for Torres is one of the first in Spanish literature to denude himself emotionally and spiritually. All the mental anguish that he feels before that natural conflict of Western man — the conflict of the flesh and the spirit — is richly expressed here. This is not to say exactly that Torres is an eighteenth-century Unamuno; yet certain aspects of his emotional writings antedate those of the twentieth-century author.

The autobiography is new in another respect also — its examination of the bourgeois mentality. It is during the 1700s that we find all kinds of works presenting the lives of quite ordinary people. Torres participates in this literary production and carries the concept further by portraying not a fictional character but a real human being, himself. In his latest study of Torres, Russell Sebold suggests that the *Life* is the creation of a very modern literary genre, the "non-fiction novel." In other words, Torres has created a "novela certificada" (to use his own words), a true story fabricated with novelistic technique. Not only is Torres a real fictional personage, he is eventually, because of his characteristics, the representative of all men of his social class in his particular time. Thus, Torres is at once a model observed, the novelist who acts as observer, and the protagonist.[20] The significant thing is that this propensity to present the bourgeois mentality is picaresque in its origin. The fight to climb socially, so important in the novel of the nineteenth and early twentieth centuries, is completely picaresque in its tone. When we find Torres in his enthralled courting of the likes of the duchess of Alba, we are witnessing a presentiment of so many bourgeois protagonists of later realistic novels. The happy consideration for us is Torres' early and unusual announcement in his own quite real life's history.

Torres' *Visions* gives us further elaboration of his philosophy of life. In direct contrast with Feijoo he believes that any past time was better than the present. While Feijoo uses the past as a model of errors, Torres preaches an impossible return to another time when Spain was more fortunate than in his own day. He sees rampant decadence everywhere. At one point he calls contemporary writers "tadpoles" — this only a short time after Feijoo's first volumes. Torres is not really an *Ilustrado* at all, a fact that has placed several critics in a dilemma as they sought to see in him a reformer as were most of the important writers of his time. Forgetting all facets of Quevedo's life and work except his morbid fascination with doom and death, Torres chooses him as the high priest of his *Visions*. He seeks to make Quevedo over in his own image. Thrusting Quevedo into his own puritanical position Torres can proceed to preach his peculiar renaissance of the Spanish spirit. He believes quite simply that the past has decayed into the present and it must be restored. The beauty of his belief is illustrated by the love he expresses for classical Spanish literature — that is, of the past. The important thing here is nevertheless his call for renovation. While it is not enlightened in tone, it is still a realization of the need for a rebirth.

The *Visions* is divided into three parts, the first published in 1727 and the two remaining in 1728. The three parts are structurally alike. That is, Quevedo appears to Torres in a dream, awakens him, and then the two wander about Madrid commenting on the various sorts of people encountered.

Torres utilizes the conceptistic style of Quevedo in his work. He adds to it a certain artistic expressionism that makes his images — and sarcasm — all the more distinct and thrusting. It is not that Torres wants to paint reality but, instead, fleeting impressions of reality as he sees it through his moralizing vision. In his extraordinary combinations of adjectives and nouns he maintains solid structure but at the same time he deforms reality through the very images and metaphors he has so cleverly wrought. We are often faced with a Daliesque sort of vision in this work that catches our attention with its near realism and then leads us into a more surreal or suprareal reality underneath. Whereas in Quevedo we are overwhelmed with the intelligence and intellectual cleverness of word combinations, in Torres the unreal artistic phenomenon is what attracts us. In essence Torres is utilizing deformation just as the expressionist does in the plastic arts of the early twentieth century. His omnipresent moralizing erupts throughout the text precisely because of this artistic style. He makes apt correlations between the deformations in language and the sins of each person. A very exact stylistic system results in which a horrible sin is described by metaphors and images of dirty, ugly things. In a way, scatology has been raised to quite artistic heights.[21]

Obviously we have only touched the surface of Torres Villarroel. The interested reader should look into much more detailed studies to begin understanding this perhaps most complex of eighteenth-century Spanish intellectuals. From our brief look, however, it is hoped that the reader can appreciate the tremendous learning, moralizing, and suffering that constituted Torres existence.

José Francisco de Isla was born in León in 1703. His parents were well educated and of some means. His mother directed his earliest studies with the help of some Jesuit fathers. Isla was a precocious child and received his *bachillerato* at the age of twelve. At fifteen he went through an abortive attempt at marriage and at sixteen he became a member of the Company of Jesus. He later studied at Salamanca, which at that time was probably at its lowest ebb. The Jesuits' own educative system saw him through what might otherwise have been a few wasted years. One of his teachers, for example, gave him a firm foundation in modern philosophy. This Father Losada assisted in the composition of Isla's *Juventud triunfante* (*Triumphant Youth*) (1727) to describe the festivals organized by the Jesuits of Salamanca in honor of St. Luis Gonzaga and St. Estanislao de Kostka, both canonized a few years previously. Isla's teaching and his preaching became renowned and his publishing continued. He also had as friends several influential national figures.

In 1754 he began to work on his most important opus, *Historia del famoso predicador Fray Gerundio de Campazas, alias Zotes* (*History of the Famous Preacher Fray Gerundio de Campazas, alias Zotes,* 1758–1768). With the expulsion decree against the Jesuits in 1767 Isla was forced to leave Spain. While traveling across the country he became ill and paralyzed, almost dying. He nevertheless insisted on continuing the journey. After many delays and vicissitudes he eventually arrived in Bologna. It was here that he made his translation of Lesage's *Gil Blas,* perhaps his most popular work after *Fray Gerundio.* He suffered another attack of paralysis in 1779 and died in Bologna in 1781.[22]

I have mentioned only a few of his works here. He was an indefatigable writer. In our study we are principally concerned with his *Fray Gerundio de Campazas.* The purpose of this satirical novel is simple. At this time the church service, especially the sermon, had become a kind of vulgar entertainment. The preaching had thus become quite overdone, full of high-blown, intellectually empty rhetoric. The degree of flamboyance of the preacher's efforts determined his and his sermon's popularity. Isla's intention was to ridicule this sort of farce to such a degree that people would truly realize its inanity and stupidity. Isla intended to return sacred oratory to its ancient dignity. He was impelled by the same motives as Luzán, who in 1737 published his *Poetics* to free poetry and drama of late Baroque decadence.

The appearance of Isla's novel was the most sensational literary event of the 1700s. Many copies were sold, from the first days. The book seemed to appeal to all types and overnight made its author a celebrity. Even the pope sent his congratulations. Just as quickly too there was much negative criticism. In spite of the protection of the court, the Inquisition suspended the printing of the second part and even the first part which had received so much acclaim. In 1760 the Inquisition condemned the book, and anyone who read or defended it was threatened with excommunication. Clandestine editions, however, continued to circulate.

This novel is one of the most outspoken anticlerical satires ever published. Isla did not limit himself to correcting Gongoristic oratory but proceeded to lambast corruption in monastic life. He says that it is just as bad to preach with flowery, empty oratory as it is to become a monk and do nothing but enjoy the good life. Isla paints man's human sins in the form of analogy. He therefore does not criticize monastic life openly, but his intentions are easily understood. Because of the sort of sly attacks the work contains many people were offended and some even feared it. The clergy naturally was horrified and roundly condemned it.

Fray Gerundio is the story of a naïve, foolishly precocious boy who later becomes a young preacher famous for his almost incredibly labyrinthine sermons. With its early humor this novel recalls the picaresque novel and even more important the first part of *Don Quixote*. In fact Isla calls it the *Don Quixote* of the preachers. We are dealing with a sort of hybrid work here. The Cervantean and the picaresque, the two outstanding novelesque developments of the *Siglo de Oro,* become fused in *Fray Gerundio*. In a vivid fashion we see the influence of Cervantes' humor on the development of the eighteenth-century novel, a development that otherwise is much more notable in England than Spain. In the 1700s the combination of picaresque and Cervantean humor was not so strange as it may appear to us, since *Don Quixote* was appreciated mainly for its lusty humor and not the more profound meanings we are expected to find in it today. The picaresque novel and *Don Quixote* are both satires and the earthiness of the two is quite the same. Seen in this light Isla's novel can be considered a continuation of the two strongest currents in the Spanish novel.

As in the case of Torres' *Life* we also find something very new in *Fray Gerundio.* Isla's descriptive technique foreshadows the development of the nineteenth- and twentieth-century realistic novel. Isla utilizes the later realistic technique in that he considers the novel a documentation of real life. The simplicity of his style seems almost a transcription of the details of a painting or, even better, life itself. This fascination with the accumulation of details is perhaps the author's most salient literary contribution. Isla's characters and episodes are made real by his taking advantage of all the possibilities of character and scene that actual life presents. His originality and literary precociousness derive from his strict observation of life, his documentation of it, and reproduction of it in his literary creation. This reproducing of life does not go beneath the surface, however. We do not necessarily find anything psychological or profound in the characters. If we remember the earlier reference to *Don Quixote,* the situation is more easily comprehensible. Fray Gerundio is a Don Quixote without his insanity. Gerundio is simply stupid, but in a comic way. Isla needed a character endowed with stupidity and errors, a figure that the seventeenth-century view of Don Quixote nicely provided.

Isla's Gerundio seems molded from the character's own environment. Fray Gerundio's ambience has "determined" him. Isla's determinism is different from that of the picaresque novel and this difference is important for his humor and his purpose. In Isla there is no concept that bad preachers are indicative of everyone or even an entire group. There are positive values in his characters and his book, which is not the case in the truly picaresque novel. Isla further affirms that this determinism results from geography. Isla would have us believe that the innocent soul of Fray Gerundio is a result of the terrain and climate. The author thus anticipates the importance of the interaction of ambience and character to the naturalists of the nineteenth century. For this reason the first "clinical" novel, that is, the naturalistic novel, may indeed be Spanish.[23]

Pedro de Montengón y Paret was born in 1745 in Alicante. He too became a Jesuit, and even though he was not a full member of the order, he went into exile. He lived essentially the rest of his life in Italy, dying in Naples in 1824. An interesting note is that he left the Jesuits after two years of exile and married. He tried to return to Spain in 1800 but soon was ordered back to Italy. He published a large number of varied works including a volume of odes, a study of Roman history, the translation or reworking of six tragedies of Sophocles, a volume of articles on scientific and historical themes, and a version of some poems by Ossian based on an Italian translation. His principal fame rests on his novels — *Antenor, Rodrigo, Mirtilo, Eudoxia,* and especially his *Eusebio.* The first two are really epic poems in prose while the *Mirtilo* is a pastoral novel. His more important *Eudoxia* and *Eusebio* are two pedagogical-philosophical novels, much in the style of Rousseau's *Émile.* [24]

The *Eusebio* is Montengón's best-known work. It appeared in four volumes between 1786 and 1788 and was not too happily received by the censors. Their alarm was due mainly to the author's insistence on expounding supposedly non-Christian philosophies, especially liberal doctrines deriving from Rousseau. The author's purpose was to make the unbelieving reader see the greater value of Christian dogma, however. The novel was finally prohibited from publication in 1798, after several printings had already been made. Montengón then revised it, but this new form was not approved until 1807, a delay of several years from his initial revision. The author also had difficulties with his famous printer Sancha. The book nevertheless did make money and this in itself is a significant attribute. *Eusebio,* with its incipient romantic expression, lachrymose philosophical dissertations, and golden, idyllic landscapes enjoyed an immense following and is the best example of the sentimental novel in the Spanish eighteenth century.

José Cadalso, the last writer of fiction to receive notice here, was born of a well-to-do family in 1741 in Cádiz. His mother died when he was quite young and his upbringing was left to maternal relatives and the Jesuits. He went to England and Europe at a very early age, and this passion for travel explains his sophistication that captured the attention of younger men such as Meléndez Valdés. By 1762 he was a cadet in a Bourbon cavalry regiment of which he was made captain in 1764. In 1766 he was made a knight of the Military Order of Santiago. His literary career began with a satire which brought about his exile from Madrid, since it was thought to be an unfavorable portrayal of the court. In 1770 he fell in love with the actress María Ignacia Ibáñez and was by this time a close friend of Jovellanos and Nicolás Fernández de Moratín. Soon he was friends with the Iriartes and Meléndez. His *Noches lúgubres* (*Mournful Nights*) and his *Cartas marruecas* (*Moroccan Letters*) were composed by 1774. In 1782 he was promoted to colonel and died in that same year during the siege of Gibraltar. [25]

The *Moroccan Letters,* first published in 1789, is an example of a type of literature very popular in the eighteenth century. Ostensibly a sort of travel literature it is actually a critique of the contemporary national scene. The best-known example is Montesquieu's *Lettres Persanes (Persian Letters).* Cadalso's work is a collection of letters sent back and forth between a young Moroccan visiting in Spain and his mentor in Morocco. Written with great verve and acumen, the *Moroccan Letters* is an outstanding example of eighteenth-century Spanish prose. Its criticism of contemporary mores, political and social decadence, and its optimistic hopes for a national sense of renewal all make it distinctive. While in a way it continues the type of criticism found in Torres earlier in the century, it lacks the latter's biting sarcasm and note of despair. It is more like the criticism of Larra and that of the Generation of '98 which, although superficially cynical, is extraordinarily positive and optimistic underneath. The following quotation from the *Moroccan Letters* reveals Cadalso's sensitivity and concern for his country:

Let the old die as they have lived and when the young of today reach adulthood, they can exhibit publicly what they now learn undercover. Within twenty years our entire scientific system would be changed without violence, and then those foreign intellectuals would see whether they have any motive for treating us with disdain.... Gradually we heard new voices and read new books which in the beginning shocked us but later only gave us pleasure. We began to read them assiduously; and as we saw that they contained a thousand truths not at all opposed to our religion or country, but indeed to laziness, we began to find other uses for our ecclesiastical books until not one of them remained. This all happened years ago ... [and we may say that] the Peninsula was sunk in ignorance in the middle of the seventeenth century and has arisen from that sea at the end of the eighteenth.[26]

As we have seen, the writing of prose in eighteenth-century Spain is quite varied in form and theme. There is much difference in subject matter and approach between Feijoo and Cadalso, for example. Yet the two have in their writing the same basic intention of reshaping the national mentality. This desire to reform is of course essential to all serious literary endeavor of the 1700s. The didactic purpose of Spanish prose during this century must therefore be understood and accepted as something vital, innovative, and generally positive.

CHAPTER 3

Eighteenth-Century Spanish Drama

I *Decadence and Reform*

TOWARD the end of the seventeenth century Spanish cultural and intellectual life declined. Just as the Great Armada of 1588 was followed by other offensive maneuvers, sometimes superficially brilliant but politically unsuccessful as international policy, so did brilliant literary production contain its own seeds of destruction and decay. For some reason poetry and drama exhibited this turnabout quite vivdly. The *cultista-conceptista* voices of Góngora and Quevedo with their appeal to a limited minority of intellectuals often evolved into vapid mouthings by weak imitators in the second half of the century. In the theater the evolutionary change was no less obvious or unexpected. By 1700 Spanish theater had degenerated into embarrassingly poor and exaggerated imitations of works by Lope de Vega and Calderón de la Barca.

The attempts at reform do not begin in 1700, however. The theater is one area where reform efforts were sporadic in the beginning and failed to achieve lasting gains until the very end of the century. This does not mean that no serious reforms were proposed nor that dramas were not written according to new proposals. The theater was an area of tremendous popular appeal and had been since the last years of the sixteenth century. If we evaluate the situation perhaps a bit too simply, we can say that the typical eighteenth-century Spaniard saw any innovation or change in attitude from the kind of plays he liked and his great-grandfather had liked as heretical, deserving of a public outcry. To the playgoer, plays were to be full of action, grand gestures, very improbable adventures and liaisons, too trusting heroines seduced by unfeeling lovers and avenged (that is, murdered) by dishonored fathers or husbands, and so on. I am not saying that the dramas of Lope and Calderón were necessarily of this ilk but that their "disciples" tended to emphasize those dramatic elements in their own plays. We remember here too that attempts by Cervantes and Juan Ruiz de Alarcón to restrain the exuberance of contemporary theater with some rules and common sense had met with little success.

Spanish theater is basically limitless. It does not want confinement. This is an excellent attribute and should not be condemned. The neoclassic reformers of the 1700s would never really try to curb this attribute. Their idea was to restrain it, to make it follow some semblance of life's reality. The purveyors of rules and the dramatists themselves of the new neoclassic school would thus always strive for a reflection of real life in their dramas. That they often became too excessive in the rigidity and dryness of their realism can be easily explained too, for this supposed rigidity in form and content was a logical reaction against what they saw as the traditionalist extreme in the other direction. The traditionalists were a strong group and fought hard and well against the efforts at reform. The traditionalist strength is seen in one of the most popular dramatists of the eighteenth century, Ramón de la Cruz, who ironically enough began his career as a neoclassicist. We shall look at him in more detail at the end of this chapter.

Really tangible evidence of reform in the theater does not occur until 1737. This milestone year, among other important literary occurrences, witnessed the publication of *La poética o Reglas de la poesía* (*Poetics or Rules of Poetry*) by Ignacio de Luzán. Although the work's immediate influence on Spanish poetry and drama continues to elicit differing interpretations, it is a valuable treatise in the development of the neoclassic mentality in Spain. Its appearance is the first determined effort to carry out reform in these two literary genres. The book in its intent is as important as Feijoo's initial publications.

Ingacio de Luzán was born in Zaragoza in 1702. His family was important, since his father was governor of Aragon at that time. This governmental position underscores the family's illustrious background and its power in regional political and social life. All this advantage to Ignacio, the youngest son, was in many ways negated emotionally by the deaths of his parents not long after his birth. The orphaned child was at first cared for by his maternal grandmother and later by an uncle who took him to Palma de Mallorca, Genoa, and Milan. These physical upheavals were occasioned by the War of the Spanish Succession which went on for the first ten years or so of Ignacio's life. His formal studies were for the most part experienced then in Italy — Milan, Naples, and Palermo. It was at the latter university that he studied law. He was also greatly attracted by the humanities, and ultimately it was this area that gave him his life's dedication. When his uncle died in 1729, he returned to Naples where his brother, a count, was governor of the castle of San Telmo.[1] He remained here until 1733 when he returned to Aragon as his brother's administrator. The rather unencumbered life he was able to lead under his brother's protection, as earlier under his uncle's, gave Luzán the opportunity for much intellectual endeavor. In 1736 he married a wealthy young woman, and in general his life continued in this somewhat peaceful, orderly way until his death.

After the publication of his *Poetics* he was made an honorary member of the Royal Academy. He moved to Madrid and soon was named full member and also member of the Academy of History. In 1747 he became secretary of the Spanish embassy in Paris, a post he held for three years. On his return to Spain other honors came his way, one of the most significant being his membership in the Academy of San Fernando. Death came to Luzán at a surprisingly early age in 1754, abbreviating a very productive and significant literary career.[2]

Even though Luzán's reputation today rests mostly on his *Poetics,* there were other literary endeavors that deserve mention. Most curious perhaps is a comedy he wrote entitled *La virtud coronada* (*Virtue Crowned*). A great deal of his work consisted of lectures given at learned functions in both Spain and Italy. These discourses or essays, as they might be more aptly termed, covered a large variety of subjects. He also composed his *Memorias literarias de París* (*Literary Memoirs From Paris,* 1751), an interesting *Carta en defensa de España* (*Letter in Defense of Spain*), and *Sobre el origen y patria primitiva de los godos* (*Concerning the Origin and Original Homeland of the Goths*). This last named and other historical treatises earned for him election to the Academy of History. All in all, Luzán is an outstanding enlightened person of the Spanish eighteenth century. He was one of those numerous limitless researchers of both superficial and profound facts. In his particular case he left us a work that served as a guide to the neoclassic evolution in Spain and established his name as the earliest arbiter of new literary directions.

In the first pages of his *Poetics* Luzán writes a few words to his readers. The instructive yet humorous style is so typical of Luzán that I include some selections from his work here. The lines very succinctly present Luzán's opinions on the status of Spanish literature and his intentions toward it:

> I had resolved, dear reader, not to tire myself or you with the weight of a prologue and for this reason I made the first chapter of my work serve as a preface. But having heard, even before the printing was finished, from various sources that people already are imputing to me what I do not say or else they are twisting my ideas with the result that I do not even recognize them, I have wanted to warn you against whatever you may hear others or even yourself say. And, first, I suggest that you not consider the rules and opinions that I propose in this work as something new and frivolous. Although they may seem so to you because they are so contrary to what the masses have usually judged and practiced down to today, I assure you that two thousand years ago these very rules were already written by Aristotle, then by Horace, commented upon by many learned and erudite men, spread among all sophisticated nations, and generally approved and followed.... Add to this that in practice and in reality, I can give them even more antiquity, it being very easy to prove that everything founded in reason is as old as reason itself.... Beyond this, what does it matter that an opinion be new as long as it is true...? Please know, dear reader, that everything I say in this work about poetry and its rules I base on sound reason and on the venerable authority of men more wise and recognized in this material....
>
> If any censure, especially concerning the plays of Calderón and Solís, seems too strong to you, I want you to know that I only relate what others have said or what occurred to me just as when Horace said similar things on seeing weak places in Homer.... And it is certain that Calderón and Solís are not the most guilty. Thus it is that the disdain with which some critics speak of our plays should rather be directed at other writers of inferior quality. This ingenuous statement of mine has seemed very necessary considering the merit of these two celebrated poets, whose genius and accomplishments I highly praise, as will be seen in various places in this book.[3]

The quotation points out certain characteristics of both Luzán and his work that in the eighteenth century were too often overlooked as they are today. First of all, his dry wit comes out nicely here. Humor is something we are told the neoclassicists eschewed because it might just reveal too much of the real, live person who had created the literary work. There is indeed a sense of humor in the Spanish neoclassicists, even though usually of a restrained nature. Another significant point emphasized in the above quotation is the importance of Spanish literature itself. Luzán's efforts to see this literature in a more universal light, even to put it on a level with that of the ancients, are exactly those of all Spanish neoclassic authors who wished to honor their nation's literary productions. And the last thing the quotation shows us is the veneration on the part of the neoclassicists for the truly outstanding authors of the Golden Age as they saw them. Luzán's *Poetics,* in addition to telling us explicitly the concepts of the neoclassic school in Spain, refutes in itself many unjust criticisms that have been made of it by contemporary and later critics.

The *Poetics* is a watershed in Spanish literature for various reasons. It of course establishes neoclassic theory in Spain. While not necessarily heeded, especially at first, and while much criticized, even today, it was always there as a guiding source for those dramatists and poets who came after and who vigorously sought an artistic renaissance. The *Poetics'* subdued but clever wit emphasizes as well the neoclassicist's basic intelligence and even compassion, a quality that has usually been denied Luzán. And, finally, the relative freedom of expression granted by him to the literary artist stresses the sophisticated capacities of the Spanish neoclassic movement.

For a more complete picture of the drama, the reader should see John Cook's *Neo-Classic Drama in Spain.*[4] The author very amply covers the vicissitudes that the reformers experienced and the reasons for their problems. On the appearance of Luzán's work certain critics felt that Spanish honor had been attacked. This phenomenon recurred throughout the century whenever the more traditionalist-minded critics felt themselves on the defensive. Such was the case noted earlier regarding Masson de Morvilliers' unfortunate comments. After 1737 many critics mounted a merciless attack upon Luzán and his ideas. Instead of praising the really good aspects of Spanish nationalist drama of the seventeenth and early eighteenth centuries and at the same time admitting its weak spots, the opposition did two things, neither one of which helped the advancement of reform. They defended the earlier Spanish theater blindly and they condemned the neoclassicists as traitors to the national honor. Second, they tried to prove for the earlier theater an already existent body of classical dramas. This was of course a none-too-subtle attempt at thwarting the reformers on their own grounds.[5]

Thus the state of the drama in the eighteenth century was not a very happy one. Although Luzán prescribed what he saw as the remedy for its illness, his precepts had little real effect. In fact, for some years they caused more bickering and pontificating than anything else. This propensity to argue plagued almost all efforts at reform and can best be understood as a psychological reaction to the guilt felt by the most outspoken defenders of the national, that is, traditionalist, drama. No real advance in imposing the neoclassical precepts was made until the reign of Charles III. As in other spheres, the firm commitment to reform by this great ruler was needed before any progress could be made.

The neoclassic reform actually began in the late 1760s under the protection of Charles' prime minister the count of Aranda. His basic aim was to make the physical appearance of the productions more pleasant and to provide the public with more and better entertainment. More important for the dramatists themselves was his decision to carry out the long-desired reform in the style of the drama. He began by soliciting opinions, and then supporting them, from the literati of the day. José Clavijo y Fajardo became the principal voice of the government's intentions. In 1762 he began to publish a journal entitled *El Pensador* (*The Thinker*), a series of essays that decried the baroque excesses of Spanish drama. Another voice, often in conflict with Clavijo's, was that of Francisco Mariano Nipho. In a different way Aranda made use of Bernardo de Iriarte, brother of Tomás. While essentially a diplomat, Bernardo dabbled in literature, and in 1765 published a translation in Spanish verse of Voltaire's *Tancrède*. In 1764 he had been elected a member of the academy. Aranda gave him the task of searching out those dramas that most closely followed classic precepts. Of some six-hundred Golden-Age plays examined Bernardo chose seventy for presentation in Madrid. He altered some of these works, however, going a little beyond Aranda's directives. He went so far as to suggest that some contemporary writers should discontinue producing their own works and merely translate French plays. He further proposed, more reasonably, that the presentation of *sainetes* between acts be abandoned and from there proceeded to a general attack on that literary genre. He felt that obscenity or baseness in any form was not to be permitted. Comedies were to be changed so as to meet the demand for verisimilitude. The unities were to be observed. He demanded the rejection once and for all of those plays containing magic, friars, or devils — in short, all those artifices of extravagance that the more vociferous elements of the audience demanded. It was basically the propensity to applaud the superficial, banal qualities of a work that most annoyed the Spanish neoclassicists. Aranda, sensing correctly that these and other suggestions might be better received outside Madrid at first, established theaters at all the royal residences. That purpose was implemented in 1768 by the establishment of the *Teatros Reales de los Sitios*.[6]

II *Tragedy*

The first real efforts at a new theater were essentially in the direction of tragedy. These first attempts often were merely translations of French plays. For example, Corneille's *Cinna* was translated before 1715. Even when dramatists followed the tenets of Lope, there was some experimentation with new methods. Antonio de Cañizares is a good example with his play *Ifigenia*. He was primarily a disciple of Lope but pursued new directions and themes. These efforts and incipient interest in more classical models and motifs should be seen at this point more as inspired by curiosity or as experimentation, for the Spanish neoclassic theater is essentially antiforeign and extremely chauvinistic, an attribute that is still often overlooked by critics vociferously attacking the eighteenth century.

It is basically Luzán's *Poetics* that turns the new dramatists toward inspiration in national figures and themes. While on the one hand it was lambasted for what some saw as its proposed antinationalistic attitude, Luzán's work did indeed propose new rules, yet supported the use of national themes. To be sure, Luzán criticized what he felt were excesses in the plays of Lope, Calderón, and their followers up into the eighteenth century. Thus, Luzán signals the essential thematic direction of Spanish neoclassic drama — a national one. His rules are meant to apply to the drama of all times and places, but while they are based on classical dictates of reason and limits, they still prefer Spanish themes.

Between 1737 and 1750, as we have implied, there is not much creative activity in the theater in Spain. More emphasis is placed on poetry by the neoclassicists, and the focus on drama is given what one may perhaps label as benign neglect. In 1749 there is an edition of several plays by Cervantes with a prologue by Blas Nasarre. He praises these works excessively and says they are much preferable to

Lope's. His reasoning here is simple, and simplistic — Cervantes followed the classical rules for composing dramas and therefore his plays are more desirable. In 1750 the first really significant work in the new theater appears. This is the *Tragedias españolas* (*Spanish Tragedies*) by Agustín Montiano y Luyando. Like Nasarre, he tries, among other things, to show how the dramatists of the seventeenth century followed the classical rules. More significant for us is the inclusion of his original work *La Virginia*. This rather fantastic piece, the first eighteenth-century Spanish tragedy to follow the rules, concerns a Roman aristocratic virgin whom the dictator intends to violate. Happily or unhappily, depending on one's point of view, her father kills her before the foul deed can be committed. Obviously there is much Calderonian intrigue and muddled psychology here at work. The principal classic motif is the Roman setting.

Montiano's second drama approaches the new concept of national theater more thoroughly. It is entitled *Ataúlfo* and deals with a Spanish Gothic king. The theme and presentation are somewhat ingenuous, but, following the ideas of the early neoclassicists, the play gives great emphasis to the classical unities.

Nicolás Fernández de Moratín actually started the serious offensive by the neoclassic dramatists. His first attempt was a neoclassic comedy entitled *La Petimetra* (*The "Elegant" Lady,* 1762). Its subtitle nicely shows the author's intentions: *Comedia nueva escrita con todo el rigor del arte* (*New Comedy Written With All the Rigor of Art*). Moratín wished to illustrate classical logic and practicality by writing a play utilizing such qualities. More important was his prologue to the play in which he emphasizes his ideas. The drama was never presented. Moratín then turned to tragedy. In 1763 he published *Lucrecia,* also preceded by a prologue stating his aims. This work received negative criticism, but the playwright, nothing daunted, wrote another (in 1770) that was mildly successful, probably only because of the protection of Aranda. This new drama was entitled *Hormesinda,* its heroine being the sister of the national hero Pelayo. From this point on we may say that Spanish neoclassic tragedy is firmly based both on classical tenets and on a nationalistic footing. If for no other reason the play is significant in making evident this valuable fact about Spanish neoclassic drama in general. Moratín wrote a third tragedy, *Guzmán el bueno* (*Guzmán the Good,* 1777). It was never presented but, as Cook notes, it established the basis for the legend utilized by later writers.[7]

There are several other writers deserving of mention for their contribution to Spanish theater, even though their importance is relatively minor. In one or two cases their work is more recognized today in genres other than the drama.

Of no great significance except for his contribution chronologically to the development of tragedy is Juan José López de Sedano. He is probably more remembered for his *Parnaso español (Spanish Parnassus).*[8] However, he wrote a tragedy in 1763 entitled *Jahel.* Like Moratín, in his preface he sets forth his ideas on the need for new dramatic technique and outlook. He is very outspoken against the exaggeration and, to his mind, the occasional indecency of the old traditional theater. Like others we have considered, Sedano hopes for a prohibition of such plays. The work is essentially a vehicle for criticism of the current stage, too traditionalist for him. It is interesting how these early writers of tragedy knew that they would have little, if any, public success and gave much attention to their prefaces or prologues, prologues at the same time aggressive in their criticism of contemporary theater and defensive in their attitudes toward their own works and probable lack of success. *Jahel* was more a private venture on Sedano's part than a revolutionary new drama, so it seems.

José Cadalso presented his tragedy *Sancho García* in 1771. It had in the role of the heroine Cadalso's lover María Ignacia Ibáñez, the leading Spanish actress of the time. Following the basic tenets of the Spanish neoclassic dramatic school, its theme was a nationalistic one. The earliest version of the theme appears in the *Primera crónica general (First General Chronicle)* of the thirteenth century. Cadalso was the first to bring it to the stage. Basically it deals with a widowed noblewoman who falls so in love with a man that she betrays her own son. Blinded by passion she becomes enamored of a Moorish king, Almanzor, and determines to help him gain her own land. As would be expected, both amorous passion and murder are thwarted and she is killed by the poison intended for her son. The guilty are thus condemned, and reason and loyalty are rightly praised.

Cadalso wrote other plays, but for the most part they are no longer extant. The dramatic fortune of *Sancho García,* however, gives us a good picture of this writer's endeavors in the theater. The play ran five days at the Cruz Theater in Madrid, beginning January 21, 1771. The small number of performances is not an indication of its lack of success; the supposedly popular Golden-Age plays usually had even more limited runs. Its failure is shown rather in the small total of box office receipts.

There is no tragic hero or heroine in this play, since the mother's demise is not caused by simple error or frailty. As Sebold well points out, the natural fear and pity expected in tragedy do not appear here. The unities are observed but this fact could not make up for other technical faults. As Sebold indicates: "there is no psychological or dramatic interest in the play."[9]

Ignacio López de Ayala wrote a grandiose tragedy in 1775, *Numancia destruida* (*Numancia Destroyed*), which was not produced until 1778. Ayala was an erudite man of his day, a professor and a member of the Academy of History. According to Cook his drama had some success, certainly more than the works we have mentioned so far. It was also produced at intervals during the next half century and was quite popular as a sort of repertory piece. The play has had to wait, as so many eighteenth-century works, until our own time for a critical edition and commentary.[10] Sebold's edition was published in 1971. The work has been roundly condemned but also praised since its appearance. The story of the doomed city besieged by the Romans is well known. The significance of Ayala's play is that while maintaining a fairly strict observance of classical rules, the author also produces much human interest. This is done through adequate character development.

Another very basic element of the play is its open chauvinism. Its theme is of course a nationalistic one, and, aside from being almost *de rigueur* in any Spanish neoclassic tragedy, it derives from Ayala's efforts to change the climate of the theater of his day. He dedicates his work to the count of Aranda, a practical political move since this government official was determined to bring about the reform of the national theater. In the play Ayala gives a great deal of emphasis to the need for concerted efforts among the Spaniards against the enemy Romans. It is apparent that the Romans were to be taken as surrogates for the enemies of enlightened reform. This purpose may be seen as compromising art but at the same time it is a definite aspect of neoclassic determination to reform and upgrade the deformed and grotesque traditionalist theater of the time.

The most significant of the neoclassic tragedies is Vicente García de la Huerta's *Raquel* (1778). The theme of this work is one of the most important in all Spanish literature, a theme perhaps as frequent as that of the Celestina or Don Juan. It first appears in the early ballads, is utilized by Lope in his *La judía de Toledo* (*The*

Jewess From Toledo), and is the subject of Mira de Amescua's better-known *La desdichada Raquel* (*The Unfortunate Raquel*), also of the seventeenth century. In 1650 Luis Ulloa composed an epic poem entitled *Raquel*. The theme has had many cultivators in various settings and languages, and the list of continuations and new versions goes on and on down to our own century.

The story of Raquel is very simple. Its simplicity allows for embellishment and moralizing in each period that the work has been popular, thus explaining the play's continuing interest. The story concerns the love of Alfonso VIII, the hero of the Battle of Las Navas de Tolosa (1212), for Raquel, a Jewish woman. The obvious intent of Huerta was to produce a play based on national history, but carefully following classical tenets, especially the three unities. For a neoclassic drama, and the first really successful one, its technique and structure come off very well. The play's major fault lies in the author's refusal to let his characters go emotionally. This is not to say that there is no human feeling in the play, because at times there is much emotional lyricism. It is rather that while wanting to write of human frailties and the resulting emotions, Huerta generally feels obligated to limit the emotional thrust of his characters, thus making them appear as pawns in his hands. If left to their own natural impulses, as it were, they would have appeared more real, albeit less "classically" restrained. What we have in this play then is an interesting neoclassic dramatic formula with strong hints of underlying romantic exuberance. It is not surprising that the neoclassic purists criticized Huerta's lack of neoclassic sensibility.

The first act begins with celebrations in Toledo because of the victory of Las Navas de Tolosa. We are introduced to Hernán García, who restrains the high emotionalism through his noble honesty and calm. He represents the loyal, honorable Castillian warrior so typical of Spanish work dealing with the Middle Ages. He is here a sort of archetypal Cid-like figure. From this point on we begin to see the problem Huerta had in balancing restraint and exuberance in his play. At the same time that this is transpiring we are introduced to Alfonso, who is torn between two extremes — love and duty. In this first act, however, he is hardly a man visibly torn by great passion for Raquel. If anything, his control is extraordinary — to the point that he calmly banishes her from his presence.

The second act presents the villain, Rubén, who works behind the scenes. Because of much psychological conflict on his own part, Rubén seeks to have Raquel take revenge on her lover. There is a great deal of argument between him and Raquel. The truly outstanding scene in the act occurs when Alfonso, after emotional and persuasive supplication on the part of Raquel, succumbs to her pleas and lifts the decree of banishment. Some of the verses of this scene reveal the strong emotion felt by the lovers. Raquel goes on her knees before the king, who in turn raises her up as she utters the following lines:

> If you think, Alfonso, that these tears,
> if you believe that these weak sighs,
> rare jewels in another time
> when better luck and Heaven ordained,
> come perhaps to act as intercessors
> between your determination and my crime. . .
> do not fear it. My tears and sobs
> are only the expression of my martyrdom,
> vapors which from my eyes has exhaled
> the flame of love contained in my heart.
> With a very opposite intention to your sight
> I return, my lord: since if before I have asked
> that you suspend the order for my exile,
> carried away by my loving delirium,
> now with better understanding I only try
> to carry out your pleasure, and I aspire solely
> in my obedience to give the last proof of my love
> with which I have always served you. . . .
> Love itself could
> learn tenderness from my emotions,
> because always your will was mine,
> and finally because adoring you
> I shall live absent, sad, and exiled. . . .

Alfonso is greatly moved by these and other words and eventually responds to her long harangue:

> But oh, how unhappy I am! What have I caused?
> Can I even think to exile Raquel?
> Can I propose it and consent to it?
> I, who breathe only at the sight of her?
> I, who live only with the faith that she loves me?
> It is not possible; neither should Heaven consent to it.
> Raquel, you will not leave: before that the thread
> of my life will be cut.

He finally reaches the height of his passion when he threatens to throw himself on his sword, proving his love for her and his disgust with his counselors who urged him to banish her in the first place:

> Noble steel, lightning bolt which brandished
> by my right hand, duplicated deeds
> worthy of powerful Mars, I dedicate you
> to a better service: be the holy
> instrument of two lovers' sacrifice.
> And you, Raquel, if you want certain and fixed testimony
> of my constant love,
> if you do not listen to my pleading, the floor
> will offer it up to you written with my blood.[11]

Alfonso's feelings of love and guilt reach such a degree that at the end of this act he places Raquel on his throne, defying anyone to question his dedication to his kingdom:

> Since there is no doubt
> and since it is my pleasure,
> know that today on my throne I substitute
> Raquel; my power and my dominion
> I transfer to her, and I myself place her
> on my royal throne; this being understood,
> since you confess to obeying me,
>   (*Placing her on the throne*)
> know that Raquel now reigns jointly with me.[12]

The defiance of Alfonso is intriguing for various reasons. He at last asserts himself in the play and becomes a more human, understandable personage. His temerity further heightens the dramatic tension that has been slowly building up in this act. In other words at this point the playwright has come to grips with the real human emotions in his work and gives them full rein. This attitude comes into conflict later with the restraint imposed upon characters and ambience in the play. Yet of all the Spanish neoclassic tragedies none achieves the magnificent emotional flights that this act of *Raquel* contains. We are witnessing a high point in dramatic effect in that theater. We must remember, however, that it is these very high-flying outbursts of unrestrained emotion that among the more puritanical-minded neoclassicists gave cause for criticism.

The final act is full of romantic bombast, all of which describes Raquel's death at the end and Alfonso's grief. He seems no less real in this act, unless it is in his realization of error at having put Raquel on the throne, allowing her to suffer at the hands of others precisely because she is a sensitive person. A certain cynicism is noted in the author's presentation of Raquel's vulnerability at this time. If any criticism is warranted, it is the failure to maintain her strong character triumphant, already seen to such good advantage in the first two acts.

The observance of the unities in this play has been criticized, but in general such criticism is superficial and, in the eighteenth century, derived from petty jealousies so common to the writers of the period. There are other questions that are of more import in the historical, dramatic sense. The conflict between Christianity and Judaism that runs underneath all the action is a significant one. In reality the characters move only in relation to this conflict, an inevitable one, as Spanish history makes so clear. While it is apparent only at times, the conflict or theme causes the personages to be essentially what they are — Alfonso weak, but eventually strong and finally contrite and Raquel, stoical and yet worldly. In neoclassic tragedy the story is always at a sort of halfway point between the freedom permitted to the novel and the more limited permissiveness of the theater. In *Raquel,* the characters are neither completely free nor completely controlled by implacable destinies. They do have an idea or presentiment about their inevitable fall, however. In dramatic tragedy the conflict between absolutes is, in great part, within the characters themselves. As a result there exists a certain autonomy within the personage himself. There is as well the expected heroic resignation before the inevitable. This is exemplified throughout the portrayal of Raquel's character. As any good tragic heroine, she does not really work to bring about her fate but rather tries to understand it. Whereas Spanish drama of the Golden Age is one offering much action and a complex plot, and action rules, the development of character is often lacking, and what we may term "well-rounded" characters are not usually to be found. In neoclassic theater everything occurs essentially within the mind of the characters, so the author usually tries to make them credible as complete human beings. Action is a relatively minor ingredient of the play. Thus we witness the characters' psychological dilemma and participate directly in the grave problems besetting them.

The psychology of Raquel is interesting in this regard. In the beginning of the play she seems a somewhat fatuous person but no less so than her lover the King. She is naïve and allows the despicable Rubén to lead her into what is ultimately to be her destruction. In this process Huerta makes Rubén the obvious villain and reduces the vapidness of the heroine. As the play develops, especially in the second act, Raquel no longer exhibits the frivolous, self-seeking demeanor exhibited earlier and becomes the noble and believable tragic heroine. She was not of noble birth, nor was she of a very old or known Jewish family. Virtue was considered the most outstanding characteristic of the truly noble, and it is precisely Raquel through her innocent vulnerability who revives the old concept of nobility. We see at work here a typically eighteenth-century idea — that is, that nobility of character that does not function does not exist, as Feijoo so well states. Once Raquel is made a noble (when she assumes the throne), she acts in a manner befitting her new status. She becomes the central figure of the play. (Except for his heroic outburst that we quoted earlier Alfonso never achieves full stature in the play.)

It is apparent from our discussion of neoclassic tragedy in Spain that it never obtained a wide audience. Much of it was simply printed and failed to achieve stage production. Most of it attracted only a minority following and this from the more intellectual devotees of the literary arts. I have mentioned that the Golden-Age plays themselves did not have as great a following as might be thought.[13] Was the appearance of Spanish neoclassic tragedy essentially just an exercise in the writing of more pronouncements on literary theory, a favorite exercise of the times as seen above? It is much more than that. In the first place, neoclassic theorists and playwrights were deeply concerned about the decadence of the theater. To be sure, their works had utilitarian motives, yet at the same time the authors considered themselves creators of a new style and world view. Their aesthetic and artistic impulse was strong. They did not necessarily think of themselves as composers for a minority, even though they attracted only a minority. Rather, they saw themselves as spokesmen for a new vision in the national theater.

I think the reason for their failure to achieve a large public lies in their reacting too strongly to what they believed an unacceptable theory of drama in the existing theater, the descendant of the baroque Calderonian and Lopean theater. As in other neoclassic manifestations, they attacked too violently without feeling the need for compromise in any area of dramatic endeavor. Their extremist fervor did lead them to choose national heroes and events for their plays, and this decision produced their most positive gift to the evolution of Spanish drama. On the other hand, this same fervor, when attacked by the traditionalists, led them to react bitterly, attacking in their own turn, and ironically with less prudence. In writing their dramas, also as a result of this fervor, they tended to restrain the action and speech of their characters. The Spanish audience, like its English counterpart, has always preferred movement and much ado on the stage. For these it had less need of reason and logic. Until the neoclassicists came to realize the need for some vitality and exuberance in what the public was supposed to accept, they had no success. This is best illustrated in the work of Huerta. His *Raquel* was fairly popular with its audiences, due to its verve and even occasional lack of realism. For this reason it serves as a culminating point in our discussion of tragedy. The fact that the neoclassic purists criticized it only further underscores the inevitability of Huerta's "faults."

III   *Comedy*

The history of neoclassic comedy in Spain is much more positive than that of tragedy. Horace's *utile dulci* could of course be more successful in comedy. The eighteenth-century neoclassic comedies were first written about the same time as the early tragedies. It was not until the late 1780s, however, that any real success was achieved with the public. The dramatist responsible was Tomás de Iriarte.

The best remembered of the neoclassic Spanish dramatists, Leandro Fernández de Moratín, wrote what may perhaps be taken as the definitive statement about his contemporary's accomplishment:

Not without some difficulty did the above-mentioned Iriarte succeed in bringing to the stage in 1788 his comedy *The Pampered Youth,* which, quite well presented by the company of Martínez, won the applause of the audience, with special attention to its moral objective, its plan, its characters, and the facility and purity of its versification and style. Perhaps it did merit the censure by those who noted its lack of dramatic movement, of levity, and of comic relief; but these defects are easily overwhelmed by the many qualities that made it estimable in both its stage presentation and its printed form. If one is to cite the first original comedy in the Spanish theater according to the rules dictated by philosophy and good criticism, it is this one.[14]

Iriarte was among those who first successfully translated foreign plays for a Spanish audience. Following his brother Bernardo's dicta we noted earlier he sought to bring about a new feeling for a restrained, reasonable theater. These plays by such writers as Destouches and Voltaire were well suited to illustrate a moral as well as provide diversion to a public too long satiated with exaggerated drivel from the stage, or so thought Iriarte and his fellow neoclassicists.

In addition to his translations Iriarte wrote at the same time his first original drama called *Hacer que hacemos* (*The Busybody*). A verse comedy in three acts, it was published in 1770 under the anagram of Tirso Imareta. Iriarte's intention was to ridicule a type of person, the busybody of the title. Naturally his basic aim was to present a play that conformed to the classical rules and taught a lesson. The plot centers around Don Gil, who is to marry Doña Elvira. Ironically, throughout the play he appears to have many more things to do than merely court Elvira. He runs hither and yon, forever talking about all he must do but never really accomplishing anything. Most of the things he is concerned with are of little consequence anyway. In the end he does not marry Elvira.

Iriarte's condemnation of Don Gil and what he represents is quite proper. The problem is that the protagonist never really becomes a person. Iriarte makes no real attempt to have the character realize how stupid and ridiculous he actually is. Without this self-knowledge Gil quite expectedly makes no attempt to reform himself. In this failure to give his character human dimension Iriarte lessens the possibility of his drama's being taken seriously. As a result it comes across very much as an empty shell, containing a message, yes, but no real profundity to the interior of that shell. This is the problem with most of the neoclassic tragedies we noted. *The Busybody* was never given stage presentation and had only the one printing in 1770, since it was not included among Iriarte's published works either in 1787 or 1805.

After the failure of his first original play Iriarte made no serious attempts to write for the stage for several years. It was during this time that he wrote more memorable works such as his *Fábulas literarias* (*Literary Fables*), which we shall examine in the next chapter. However, he retained a desire to write a successful play that would put into effect his ideas about what the new theater should be. It was taken for granted that the work would have to teach, to have a moral. The greatest difficulty would be to present a type who in his general makeup would be believable and therefore acceptable to the public. Iriarte chose well this time. *El señorito mimado (The Pampered Youth)* concerns the pampered, spoiled son of an indulgent mother. The play was written in the early 1780s, printed in the complete works in 1787, and produced in September, 1788, to a thunderous reception.

A verse drama in three acts, the play illustrates what happens to a dissipated, naïve youth. Oddly, however, it does not condemn the son so much as it faults his mother. This theme of proper education of the young is popular with all neoclassic writers and their disciples and is found everywhere from Iriarte to Larra. The foolishness of the mother is emphasized everywhere in the play and at the end, when Mariano is sent away by his uncle, we are to understand that he is essentially being removed from his mother's obsessive overprotection to attempt an independent life of his own. The moral is nicely underlined in the uncle's lines: "Begin to live again from this point on. You fully realize the state into which laziness, ignorance, and the habits of a bad education have catapulted you.... What? You become confused? That is not a bad sign. With that, if you some day have children, you can cite them this example, and if you do not better instruct them, what is happening to you today will also happen to them."[15]

Concurrent with the success of *The Pampered Youth,* Iriarte published in 1788 another play, *La señorita mal-criada (The Ill-Bred Miss)*. It was not produced until 1791. It too is in three acts and in verse and is a variation on the theme of *The Pampered Youth*. Here it is the father who spoils his willful daughter. Because of the parent's indulgence Pepita has no sense of obligation to anyone or anything but herself. She is totally humiliated, and reason completely triumphs over self-indulgence when the father proclaims at the end of the play: "...henceforth I shall learn to be more cautious; and let other careless fathers learn from my example."[16]

Iriarte wrote other comedies but none with the success of these two. This success derived from something he failed to achieve in *The Busybody* — a sense of balance. Balance is nowhere better seen than in the characters themselves who relay the drama's message to us. We react here not to the wooden figures of his first play but to real human beings. While each character in the two successful plays represents some moral weakness or strength, he at the same time possesses qualities that set him off as a realistic living person. The secret of Iriarte's success, his sense of balance, had behind it a further secret therefore — his full comprehension of the truth in Horace's *utile-dulci* concept: gentleness.

Before leaving Iriarte we must mention one further contribution of his to the Spanish stage. That is the *melólogo* or melologue introduced from France where it had begun with Rousseau. Iriarte wrote the first really popular melologue in Spanish: *Guzmán el bueno, Soliloquio ú escena trágica unipersonal, con música en sus intervalos (Guzmán, The Good, Soliloquy or Tragic Scene for One Person, With Music in its Intervals)*. It was printed in 1790 and appeared on the stage only a few months before Iriarte's death in 1791. The play has no real plot but is essentially a study of that venerated figure in Spanish history and literature, Alonso Pérez de Guzmán, who in the thirteenth century sacrificed his son rather than betray his word to his king. Iriarte's short drama presents the emotional crisis of the father in the moments before his son's death. Guzmán experiences many emotions as he wrestles with his conscience. The scene is very credible, and the dilemma of the father is portrayed in a quite realistic, acceptable fashion. The injection of music between and during the scenes, and particularly during the father's final monologue, heightens the effect upon the audience to a considerable degree. The resultant evocation of emotion is extraordinary and the audience's reaction must have been one of absorbed participation, thus creating a more immediate and lasting reaction than other treatments of this same theme in longer plays.[17]

Iriarte represents the beginning of the successful apex of neoclassic comedy in Spain. We shall return to its history more specifically, but for the moment note must be made of a very important antecedent in the seventeenth century. In the 1600s there was one dramatist who did not follow the route of Lope and Calderón. This was Juan Ruiz de Alarcón (1581–1639). His theater stresses moral issues more strongly than most playwrights of his time. The quantity of his work is not large, for he wrote only twenty-seven plays, of which no more than twenty were printed. Whereas Lope and his school wrote principally to entertain the public, Alarcón wrote to entertain and to instruct it, to lift its moral outlook. As a consequence he was not as well loved by the public or his fellow dramatists.

The tone of his theater is essentially that of the eighteenth-century neoclassicists. The plots of his plays are generally simple, slowly and carefully developed, and the language is precise. Passion is not given highly emotional expression in Alarcón's plays; he tends more toward logic and reason. He wrote several types of drama. The most lasting and best known is his so-called *comedia de carácter,* of which the two most popular are *La verdad sospechosa* (*The Suspicious Truth*) and *Las paredes oyen* (*The Walls Have Ears*). In this type of play the protagonist represents some human defect that is roundly condemned. Just as in the plays of Iriarte he is ridiculed in front of everyone, and the public's morals are stressed in the hope that people will be edified.

Alarcón's works have a tone that is not characteristic of the seventeenth-century Spanish theater. Alarcón and Cervantes present the most forthright attempts to restrict the often overdone exuberance of the theater of their day. Cervantes' influence on dramatic practice was minimal. Alarcón had some influence on foreign writers, especially Molière. In his turn the latter then influenced the eighteenth-century Spanish neoclassicists such as Leandro Fernández de Moratín. My intention in this digression on Alarcón is to make clear the continuity in the evolution of neoclassic drama in Spain. The major thrust of the neoclassic fervor in the theater is evident from about 1770 to 1800, and, it would seem, had its origins in Spain itself and was not an unnatural outburst as some critics since the 1700s have insisted.

The most accomplished writer of neoclassic comedy was Leandro Fernández de Moratín. He is often referred to as Moratín, *hijo* ("junior"), since he was the son of Nicolás Fernández de Moratín, a writer of neoclassic tragedy. Leandro was born in Madrid in 1760. As in other neoclassic writers of this period, his literary inclinations became evident while he was in his teens. In 1779 he received a prize awarded by the Royal Academy of the Language for his poem "La toma de Granada" ("The conquest of Granada"). The work itself demonstrates once more the interest of the neoclassicists in national themes. His father, who was also a jeweler of great talent, tried to encourage him to take up that more lucrative trade, remembering the difficulties that he himself had encountered in the theater. After the death of his father in 1780 Leandro did work as a jeweler until about 1786, but after that time he no longer followed it as an occupation. In 1782 his didactic poem "Lección poética" ("Poetic Lesson") received a prize from the Royal Academy. The work discusses the literary excesses of his day. His mother died in 1785 and a year later he read his first comedy *El viejo y la niña* (*The*

Old Man and the Young Lady) to the company of Manuel Martínez.

As we can see, Moratín's work was taking a definite direction toward the theater by this time and away from the more practical spheres that his father had envisioned for him. Nevertheless, he became involved in various schemes that made him known to a wide variety of people. In January, 1787, he was named secretary to the count of Cabarrús and accompanied him to France where he remained some eleven months. It was here that he wrote a *zarzuela* called *El barón* (*The Baron*). Two years later he took religious orders, becoming an abbé and hoping to receive a benefice from the church. He also published in 1789 his well-known prose satire *La derrota de los pedantes* (*The Defeat of the Pedants*). In 1790, after a hiatus of four years, his first play was at last produced to a mixed public response. In 1792 one of his two most famous plays, *La comedia nueva o el café* (*The New Comedy or the Café*), was produced.

Between 1792 and 1796 he was in various European countries. He went first to France, sent there on some minor mission by the prime minister Godoy. Because of the increasing chaos in France he fled to England where he stayed almost two years. This was a fruitful period for him. He learned English and began to study Shakespeare and English drama in general, a project that made him even more conscious of the background of Spanish drama and the value of its often uneven, exaggerated temperament. Between 1793 and 1796 he was in Italy where he seems to have preferred the city of Bologna for his principal residence.

He returned to Spain in 1796 when he was named the secretary of the interpretation of languages. In 1798 his prose translation of Shakespeare's *Hamlet* was published. In 1803 his play *The Baron* was produced in Madrid. It was followed a year later by *La mojigata* (*The Prudish Lady*). The second of his two best-loved plays, *El sí de las niñas* (*The Agreement of the Young Ladies*), was produced in 1806 to an enthusiastic audience.

In 1808 he fled Madrid, along with other artists, trying to avoid the invading French troops. Like many he soon returned to take up a government position, this time under Napoleon's brother, Joseph Bonaparte. In 1811 Joseph named him librarian of the Royal Library. In 1812 his version of a play by Molière was produced, *La escuela de los maridos* (*The School for Husbands*). Ironically he was forced to leave Madrid this same year as the Bonaparte forces gave ground to the allies. He was never to return to the capital. He first went to Valencia where the Bonaporte forces had set up a sort of provisionary government. In 1813 he went with the remainder of the French contingent to Peñíscola. From 1814 to 1817 he was able to live quietly in Barcelona, not immediately suffering exile. Self-imposed exile did come about nevertheless between 1817 and 1820. Moratín feared the Inquisition, zealous in its persecutions of questionable citizens, and lived in France for these three years. He returned to Barcelona in 1820. A year later he returned to France while trying to escape the plague. In 1827 he moved to Paris where he died the next year.[18] Like others of the *Ilustrados* who tried to make peace with the governments of both Charles IV and Joseph, Moratín spent the last years of his life seemingly indecisive in his political stances. Like them too, however, he was attempting to follow some sort of sense in government. His unfortunate flights and exiles in his final years only heighten his inability to achieve that reason in his public life that he so very much desired.

In general, Moratín's work represents a challenge to the traditionalist outlook and in its entirety had positive and successful results. We shall look at only two of his plays here. *The New Comedy or the Café* sets out to satirize the excesses in the theater of the day. Don Eleuterio has composed an elaborate drama entitled *El cerco de Viena (The Siege of Vienna)*, which in its incredible scenes and general lack of discipline quite well reflects some popular contemporary plays. In fact, the partisans of these latter attempted to attack Moratín's play as libelous. It is both somewhat amusing and sad to realize how successful Moratín was being in his portrayal of corruption in the theater. The success of Don Eleuterio's play is necessary if he is to solve his financial problems and also work out a satisfactory marriage of his sister to Don Hermógenes, one of the funniest dramatic creations of the century. As we would expect, Eleuterio's play is a disaster and, as in other neoclassic dramas, a sensible older gentleman appears at the end to lecture the fledgling dramatist and his audience on the foolishness of such writers and their silly dramas. He also very kindly offers financial salvation to Don Eleuterio, and the play thus terminates on a happy, healthy note for all those who were knowingly or unknowingly pursuing the wrong ends.

The Agreement of the Young Ladies deals with a popular theme in the eighteenth century — the needed independence of young people. This theme is indirectly reflected in Iriarte's two plays that we noted, for had it not been for the lax behavior of the parents there, the children would have much earlier learned to behave themselves and mature normally. In Moratín's play it is the heroine's fatuous mother Irene who is largely to blame for the "problem" of the drama. As the work begins, Paquita has left the convent where she has been educated and is now en route to marry a much older gentleman, Don Diego, whose money and social position her mother covets. Paquita is in love with Don Diego's nephew, Don Carlos, whom she calls upon to prevent the wedding. Carlos, a soldier, leaves his post and joins his beloved in the inn where all the action occurs. However, when he discovers that his uncle is the proposed bridegroom, he reluctantly withdraws. His love and respect for his uncle are thus nicely underscored. Passion, we are to understand, must at times give way to honor and duty. Fortunately the sensible old gentleman realizes the foolishness of the proposed marriage. This realization is perhaps a bit tardy since for some time he has been exposed to the mother's greed and social ambition and the daughter's reluctance. At any rate, he withdraws and delivers a sensible lecture to us all.

Moratín's plays are more than simple commentaries on people and their foibles. They are much more too than criticism of literary and human excesses. Moratín's plays are a refinement in the form and message of Spanish comedy. In his dramas he writes with great verve using the *romance* ("ballad form") as his basic meter. The classical unities are carefully followed, but this does not mean an overall rigidity in dramatic concept. In *The Agreement of the Young Ladies,* for example, the author ingeniously chooses a hallway for the presentation of the play's action. This hallway has doorways leading outward, creating the illusion of more space. The intelligence of Moratín's choice of location is a small stroke of genius. He uses a similar device in his *The New Comedy.* This play's action occurs in the café on the stage, but from the floor above we hear noise and chaos that expand our concept of space. In another sense, the noise symbolically prepares us for the disaster of Eleuterio's play.

The message of Moratín's plays is the need for reason, reason in literature and in every aspect of life. There is a call for common sense in dealing with conflicts, whether they be personal or societal. Moratín's dramas then possess more depth than those of any other dramatist of his time. Beneath the ridiculousness of a Doña Irene or a Don Hermógenes we see reflections of the sad state of affairs both in and outside Spain in the late 1700s and early 1800s. The author is counseling prudence in the everyday lives of his audience, but he is also urging reason and logic on the government as it attempts to guide the nation through difficult waters. None of this advice is overt, but it comes across to the audience or reader through the pervasive atmosphere of common sense and intelligence. As no other playwright of his time Moratín gives us the Horatian dictum of *utile dulci* in a sophisticated manner that still appeals today.

A further contribution of the *Ilustrados* to the drama of the period is the *comedia sentimental* ("sentimental drama"). Much like the melologue its vogue occurs principally at the end of the century and is best represented by a work of Jovellanos. His *El delincuente honrado* (*The Honorable Delinquent,* 1773) is usually referred to as the prime example of the genre in Spain. The sentimental or tearful drama (*la comédie larmoyante*) began in France. Luzán even translated one into Spanish so this type of play was in vogue quite early in the century. The principal purpose of the genre was to move the spectator or reader to great emotion, particularly tenderness and compassion. We can see in these emotions a very early romantic aura. The aim of arousing strong emotion reflects that of the melologue, although, as seen above, this sort of play was much more brief and was accompanied by music. The sentimental drama was also didactic, a characteristic expected in the Enlightenment. Often the theme was so emotionally presented that the characters were nearly overwhelmed by it.

The Honorable Delinquent has more than a touch of this element. Jovellanos created the play almost on a dare to show that such writing could indeed offer both entertainment and instruction. The play's purpose is to reveal the harshness of certain laws, in this case those regarding the art of duelling wherein both duellists were punished without considering which of the two was really responsible. The plot is very simple and perhaps more than a little maudlin. The hero, Torcuato, kills a vile man in a secret duel after having refused to fight him several times before. He eventually marries the man's wife, Laura, whom he has loved for some time. A friend of Torcuato, Anselmo, is arrested as the one responsible for the murder. When Torcuato finds out what has happened, he confesses and is then sentenced to death by a very proper judge, Don Justo. All this is not unduly farfetched or unreasonable. The remainder of the play does become so, however. The judge who has always felt very kindly toward Torcuato is discovered to be his real father. He had never before known this son whom he had fathered illegitimately. After Anselmo is saved by Torcuato's confession, he seeks an act of pardon from the king. The pardon is granted and all ends happily for the "delinquent" and his friends.

The point of the play is obvious, for the enforcement of the duelling law is condemned. Don Justo metes out justice according to that law, but he also feels that it is unjust. The lack of distinction between the two parties involved in the duel and the fact that society itself approved of duelling as an acceptable method to avenge one's honor are great concerns of Don Justo. His philosophical musings through the play are important in stressing the author's thesis. Don Justo's human weakness in never knowing his own son further heightens his significance as an arbiter of truly sensible justice. It is noteworthy that although he follows the law to the letter, he nevertheless preserves his integrity as a judge. Jovellanos' forgiveness of him as both a poor father and his approval of him as a basically humanitarian judge through the king's pardon only stress the "sentimental" aspect of the work while emphasizing its thesis very forcefully.

The play's early romanticism has been duly noted by John Polt.[19] The melodramatic tone is found throughout and anticipates the overdone and exclamatory emotionalism of romantic dramas of the 1830s. As Polt aptly points out, Torcuato is a very good antecedent of Don Álvaro in the duke of Rivas' well-known nineteenth-century drama. The illegitimate son of an unknown father who against his will commits an illegal act, who must hide his guilt from his wife and then separate himself from her as a consequence of this guilt, and who finally must condemn himself to save a friend is an excellent example of the hero pursued by what seems to be a relentlessly evil fate. The difference of this play from a tragedy, however, is its emphasis on the essential goodness of the hero and his triumphing over that fate. This is brought about in great part, perhaps ironically, by the moralistic theme that Jovellanos is determined to project. By moving his viewer to tears, as it were, he expects to get across the neoclassic didacticism — something the neoclassicists in their tragedies were unable to do with any degree of success.

There were other examples of the sentimental genre in Spain. In general they were translations of works that had enthusiastic audiences in other countries. While somewhat different in tone from other neoclassic dramatic fare, they nevertheless were an integral part of the *Ilustrados'* attempt to create a better, more uplifting theater in Spain, especially in the second half of the eighteenth century.

IV *Traditionalist Theater*

The world "traditionalist" is used somewhat loosely in this section. It refers essentially to all the theater that is not of the neoclassic school. As a result it can include a variety of plays, from the most exaggerated of the old baroque school to the popular *costumbrista* theater of Ramón de la Cruz.

We have noted before the popularity of the plays of the Lopean school. Some critics today tend to doubt the great claims for their popularity, however. There is no question that many of those old dramas did enjoy the public's attention and were presented throughout the century. It was against the most flamboyant aspects of these plays that the neoclassicists directed their jibes. There were playwrights too who feigned reform in their works but still filled them with sensationalism and spectacular action. The problem of teaching the public and yet giving the public what it seemed to want was a difficulty for all the dramatists of the time. The question of public taste of which the neoclassicists saw themselves as the arbiters was thus of extreme importance in the theater. Often it is the manner in which the more traditionalist writers approached this question that determined how the plays were composed and also whether they were accepted or rejected by the public. All the dramatists, even the strictest neoclassicists, made concessions to what they considered poor public taste. In a not too farfetched example, Moratín, by telling us something of what is in Don Eleuterio's ridiculous play, has indeed inserted in *The New Comedy* the very excesses that he condemns. In this he was exercising a major function of satire.

The New Comedy is of interest in its attack on the popular exaggerated plays being written at that time. Moratín is condemning in Don Eleuterio's play a work that ostensibly follows neoclassic dictates but sins by trying to titillate its audience by overdone appeals to its senses. He was probably criticizing more than any others of his time the popular dramatist Luciano Francisco Comella. Comella, who lived from 1751 to 1812, achieved a phenomenal success with the public, and in his short-lived popularity was not unlike Echegaray a century later. While on the one hand professing to be interested in reform of the theater, on the other he filled his plays with fantastic plots, mass movements of people on the stage, multiple changes of scene, and other similar devices to arouse the public's basic human urges. When Moratín's play was presented, it was generally viewed as an attack on Comella, specifically, on a work entitled *El sitio de Calés* (*The Siege of Calais,* 1790).

There were others too who sought to attract a public through spectacle instead of reason, sensibility, and virtue. In many cases, even though their excesses seemed to imitate the worst of the Golden-Age productions, they were following dictates of their own which in turn were based on the increasing emotionalism in the theater. Both the sentimental drama and the melologue attest to this new phenomenon although in a more reserved and respectable way. At the same time one must be sure not to criticize these minor playwrights too severely. In the first place, they were indeed popular with the public. It was only Moratín who among the more seriously reform-minded was able to achieve true popularity. Second, those playwrights did attempt to bring about certain reforms. Their emphasis on excessive dramatic effect was what distinguished them from their compatriots. A new look should be, and is being, taken at Comella and his school. He is not deserving of the severe condemnation he has received.

By far the most popular dramatist of the second half of the eighteenth century was Ramón de la Cruz. His was an intriguing career. Beginning as a neoclassic writer interested in the reforms that that school proposed, he eventually found his greatest success in the popular *sainete,* a one-act play portraying contemporary types of people and places. The *sainete* had its beginnings in the sixteenth century in the *paso,* popularized by Lope de Rueda. The original intent was to provide entertainment for the rowdy audiences of the day during the breaks between the acts of longer plays. This sort of drama had to be quick-paced, funny, and easily understandable to its audience. From these rather low beginnings the *paso* developed in the seventeenth century into the *entremés,* of which the two most famous writers were Cervantes and Quiñones de Benavente. By the end of the eighteenth century this dramatic genre had become a permanent fixture of the Spanish stage. It met with vicissitudes throughout its history. Ironically it was the neoclassicists who most opposed it for its lack of verisimilitude. This was an unfair criticism, since it did portray social types in a believable way. The lack of taste in these little plays was what most disturbed the neoclassicists. The depiction of a certain degree of reality, as I have indicated, was the genre's strong point. This sense of the contemporary scene was necessary in these plays, and, as a result, we may say that the real beginnings of the *costumbrista* movement of the 1820s and 1830s are to be found in the *sainete*.

Ramón de la Cruz was born in 1731 in Madrid. Unlike the parents of some of the younger neoclassicists, his were of moderate means, and it was only through the help of more distant relatives that he received his early schooling. Fortunately the boy himself was very intelligent and did well in his studies. At the age of thirteen he wrote his first poetry and a short time thereafter his first plays. He later married. In 1759 he began his long bureaucratic career in the government. Evidently he never had much financial success, even though he did enjoy the protection of the duke of Alba and the countess of Benavente, in whose house he died in 1794. He suffered from poor health, and the costs of his illness were a great burden on the family. The countess of Benavente granted a pension to his wife and his daughter after he died. This occurred after his widow had to go begging of his former employers. It would appear then, as in so many other instances of literary misfortune, that Cruz did not gain much wealth from the tremendous popularity of his plays.[20]

I note one *sainete* here, *Manolo,* one of Cruz' best known. It is a fascinating, quick-paced little play that has a captivating flippancy throughout. Its subtitle reads: *Tragedia para reír o sainete para llorar* (*Tragedy for Laughter or Sainete for Crying*). There are twelve very short scenes filled with music, conversation, and general boisterousness, all taking place in a public street in front of a tavern. From the very beginning we see the *sainete's* purpose of reflecting life as it daily occurs.

There is a simple plot. Tío Matute has a daughter Remilgada, whom he intends to marry to Manolo, a somewhat wild young man who has been off to foreign parts for the last ten years. We are given to understand that he did not go off of his own accord but was arrested and deported. The rough but human tone of Cervantes' galley slaves is recalled in Manolo's worldly-wise, humorous attitude. He has today returned home where he finds his father dead and his mother married to Tío Matute. Neither one of the intended newlyweds seems very happy with the decision to marry them. Complicating the situation even further, Potajera appears in order to claim Manolo's promise of marriage given before he went away. Manolo does not wish to marry her. Mediodiente ("Half-tooth," a delightful name certainly that conjures up quite well the low-life ambience we are witnessing), declares himself the defender of Potajera's honor and calls Manolo out. A terrific fight ensues within the tavern which we only hear from outside. The fight is so severe that all the participants are eventually killed. However, we are not to take any of this too seriously. Cruz presents us with two final scenes that in their flippancy and almost surrealistic tone anticipate our contemporary theater of the absurd. Ionesco's *La Cantatrice Chauve* (*The Bald Soprano*) immediately comes to mind in the absurdity of the lines below. As first Manolo falls down — a travesty of the ill-fated hero — and then his mother, Tío Matute falls dead, saying: "I also want to die / so as not to fight or pay funeral costs." Remilgada, on seeing her father's demise, cries out: "I am going to die right away." She promptly does and is followed immediately by Potajera.

The final scene is the culmination of the ridiculous:

SABASTIAN:	As for us, shall we die or what?
MEDIODIENTE:	Friend, it is either "trigedy" or not "trigedy":
	it is necessary to die; writers should only
	pardon the life of him
	who has the most gloomy face
	in order to give the final statement.
SABASTIÁN:	Well, you give it and note that I have died
	from laughter.
MEDIODIENTE:	I too. How does all your work benefit you,
	laborers,
	to alleviate your weekdays of misery,
	if by Sunday or Monday
	you have wasted your wages in the tavern?[21]

One can well imagine the horror of the neoclassicists at the portrayal of such low types, their living conditions, and colloquial speech. In this particular play the mockery of the protagonist by Cruz would have been even more unpalatable to them. Neither would they have accepted the absurdity underlying the entire play which comes completely to the surface in the final scene. And yet we today must look to the results on the audience. Undoubtedly the general public found this entertainment most diverting. Individuals could see themselves, their family, and friends mirrored in one or more of the very ordinary characters. They could laugh at the absurdities that these latter both were and projected. Cruz, then, captivated his audience, and once having done so his method did not matter. He was at that point to do with it whatever he wanted. And what he wanted was to instruct as well as entertain. Mediodiente's short harangue at the end follows Horace's dictum quite nicely. In its import and in its final presentation, the message is fundamentally the same as that found in the best literary production of the neoclassic school, the *Literary Fables*.

Cruz' *Manolo* provides a good conclusion for our chapter on the theater. As in all literary genres in eighteenth-century Spain, there was much attempt at reformation. The outright efforts were not often successful as we saw in the case of neoclassic tragedy. The traditionalist theater often was diametrically opposed to the reforms, but such opposition does not mean that neoclassic urge for change did not influence it. *Manolo* attests to this pervading influence and shows us once more that Spain in this enlightened century did not always follow certain other European patterns for change. Yet the desire for change and change itself were always there.

CHAPTER 4

Poetry

I *Background*

L IKE the other literary genres, poetry was also in a state of decline as the eighteenth century began. The disciples of the old
Gongoristic-conceptistic school of the preceding century were very
much in evidence. In fact, the initial decadence of poetry and the
effort at its reformation are the most visible occurrences in the
literature of this period. The changes in attitudes throughout the
century serve today as a guide to understanding what the main
problems were in the literary stagnation and the basic attempts to
undo that stagnation. For this reason I have saved our discussion
of poetry until the end because its gradual metamorphosis in itself
is a good review of much that we have said earlier about other
genres and attitudes in general during the 1700s.

The neoclassic movement, that is, the reformation, in poetry
does not have much effect until after the middle of the century.
And all during the second half the fight is a prolonged and agonizing one for many writers. As in other genres the traditionalist
mentality in poetry is too strong to be easily overwhelmed. For over
one hundred years inadequate poetic expression had been the rule,
and any effort for change was belittled and resented by the literati
and the public. The influence of Góngora's verses, clever but too
empty of meaning, aesthetically exquisite but too difficult for comprehension, had held sway since his death prior to 1650. Quevedo's
conceptistic poetry had held on in the same way. The appeal of
these two poets to a definite minority had so prolonged itself with a
general public that by 1700 and later accepted poetic expression was
of necessity convoluted and ambiguous.

To see a little better what this sort of poetry was we shall look briefly at three poets of the first half of the century. Gabriel Álvarez de Toledo was born in 1662 and died in 1714. Very little would be known of his life had not Torres Villarroel published Álvarez de Toledo's works and provided a biography. Given the personality of Torres, however, one cannot be sure that all that he says about the poet is true. The *Bosquejo histórico-crítico de la poesía castellana en el siglo XVIII* (*Historical-Critical Outline of Spanish Poetry in the Eighteenth Century*) in the *Biblioteca de Autores Españoles* (*Library of Spanish Authors*) conveniently cites Torres for us.[1] Supposedly the poet's first years were somewhat dissipated until he suffered a conversion to a more stable sort of life. He became pious, political, and literary — quite a combination for one person certainly. He held high posts in the government and helped found the Royal Academy. He was one of the most erudite Spaniards of his time. By no means did he belong to the Enlightenment that was beginning in his final years. His religious fervor and his patriotic sense combined very well to make him an excellent disciple of the old baroque school of the seventeenth century, that is, that of Quevedo, Góngora, and Calderón.

For the most part Álvarez de Toledo's poetry reflects his sober, moralistic outlook on life. One sonnet in particular illustrates this outlook very succinctly in its reflection of baroque attitudes. The poem is entitled "A Roma destruida" ("To Rome Destroyed"). The glory of ancient Rome and her decay fascinated the baroque mind, so preoccupied was it with death and inevitable destruction. Paintings of the period vividly portray this morbid fascination, but it was a visible attribute of all artistic expression. This brooding upon the decay of life and the unavoidable abyss of the hereafter (whatever that might turn out to be) at times included an attitude of flippancy and sophisticated cynicism in many artists. Góngora often exhibits an undeniable fatalism in his work. Sor Juana de la Cruz captures it perhaps better than anyone in the sonnet inspired by her portrait. In the poem now quoted from Álvarez de Toledo the fascination is still here, but there is also a tone of admiration as well. I think it is this latter tone that sets this poet somewhat apart from the earlier baroque school. While it does not indicate any really new attitude to be continued later in the eighteenth century, it does emphasize the possibility for innovation in attitudes at least:

You fell, haughty Rome, at last you fell,

you, who when elevated to the Heavens,
did not deign to be leader of the world
because you chose to be the world itself.
　　What a proud edifice you erected,
with no less astonishment you hurled yourself down,
since you stretched yourself into all spheres of the world,
oh, Rome! and yet only in yourself could you fit.
　　Establishing eternal glory in what is transitory,
your corpse reduced to dust
will be a witness of your victory,
　　because just being what you were,
neither can time erase your memory,
nor your ruin fit into oblivion.[2]

The idea that Rome has not been destroyed for her past sins and that her ruins elicit veneration is outstanding in this poem. The writer does not want us to forget that indeed Rome has been destroyed. Yet what remains of the ancient civilization is to serve more than simply as a moral guide. We are to appreciate the ruins for what they once were, something noble and magnificent. The poem's double call to learn and to admire is not so very far from Horace's dictum.

Eugenio Gerardo Lobo was born into a noble family in 1679. At an early age he entered the military where he enjoyed a brilliant and heroic career. He took part in the Spanish War of Succession and participated in battles in Africa and Italy. His honors were numerous. He was made a member of the Order of Santiago and was both military and civil governor of Barcelona. While actively involved in the military life, he still found time to write, mostly poetry but also some plays. He died in 1750 after falling from his horse.

Lobo was a cultured man and his poetic compositions reflect his sophistication. The poetry that is considered his best today, however, possesses a personal attitude that calls to mind a man who could express his inner feelings honestly and openly. The poet himself seems to have intended this sort of verses mainly for his own diversion and self-expiation. He refused to publish these poems, although some were printed without his permission in 1717. He himself did finally authorize the appearance of another collection, but it was not until after his death that a more adequate publication was made.

One sonnet gives us some idea of the potential baroque flippancy of Lobo. Its Petrarchan theme of withered love, so beloved since

Garcilaso's day, is essential to the poem's structure and meaning, yet in its necessary bitterness and disillusion the theme is softened by a sort of languid resignation. The word "languid" is significant here, for it connotes a new feeling more typical of the eighteenth century, a feeling not unlike that in rococo art. The baroque artist would have been too bitter to feel languid:

> A trunk denuded of green branches [you are],
> which was a leafy refuge in another age
> and today you suffer the rigors of cold January
> the drier the wetter [you are].
>   Happy you, who in that poor state
> still live happier than I in mine;
> unhappy I, who sad distrust
> being envied by another.
>   That pomp which is now withered,
> in that other flowery time waited
> for the flowers and the trees to revive.
>   The year forms its cycle, and flattering
> spring visits us all;
> only for my love there is no spring.[3]

The Petrarchan theme becomes almost an afterthought. The sensation of emptiness and resignation is much more important. Whereas Garcilaso, for example, would have also appeared resigned to fate, he would nevertheless have bemoaned that fate to a much greater degree. Lobo is more human, more natural, as it were. It is this naturalness of his poetry that captivates the reader today. This naturalness is especially visible in his longer poems written to individual friends. It is also quite apparent in such playful verses as the "Letrilla: A una viuda moza y rica, llorando sin consuelo la muerte de su marido" ("To a Young and Rich Widow, Bewailing the Death of Her Husband"). Sample lines give some idea of its tone:

> If you do not pretend pain,
> tell me, why do you cry?
>   If losing a husband,
> we see you, Nise, crying,
> and there is nothing easier
> to arrange than a marriage,
>   tell me, why do you cry? . . .
>   If John reposes in Heaven

(God knows where he reposes),
and you have who may ask God
to grant you His glory,
    tell me, why do you cry?
Well then, dear Nise,
either you are a fool,
or if you do not pretend,
    tell me, why do you cry?[4]

Lobo has left us the more human side of traditionalist poetry. We see reflected the attitude of a Quevedo, even a Góngora, in their more teasing moods. The emphasis is not so much on word games as on playfulness. Thus Lobo continues certain aspects of the baroque mentality but, as seen, he also inserts a human compassion in his work which could not be so easily expressed beneath the old baroque surface of cynicism and disillusion. Lobo announces for us very early, although admittedly none too strongly, the rococo attitude that is best seen in the poetry of Meléndez Valdés in the second half of the century.

We have already examined the prose work of Torres Villarroel but now we must note his poetry. We also looked at his rather exuberant life as seen in his "autobiography." Because of his prose writings and his great popularity as an outspoken critic of his day, his prose work has received more attention than his poetic endeavors. His poetry, as we might expect from his flamboyant prose, owes much to the conceptistic influence of his seventeenth-century mentor Quevedo. There is much philosophical and amorous poetry by Torres, but for the most part it is his satirical verse that has meaning for moderns. The precise concision of his satirical poetry is illustrated in the following sonnet entitled "Ciencia de los cortesanos de este siglo" ("Science of the Courtiers of This Century"):

To bathe with flour one's hair,
to go showing everyone one's underclothing,
one's sword that does not frighten and causes laughter,
one's ring, one's watch and its chain;
    to speak to everyone with a calm countenance,
to kiss Doña Luisa's feet at mass,
and to give oneself regularly
to condolences, to pleasure, and to congratulations;
    to be in love with oneself,
to mumble a short tune in Italian,
and to dance in French right or wrong;

>   with this, and to forget the catechism,
>   there ready and made are you the courtier,
>   but the Devil will carry you off.[5]

The language here is not so clever and bitter as Quevedo's might be, but the moralistic tone is the same. There is more to the tone of course than its simple moralizing, however. One feels the anger and bitterness of the writer when looking at the contemporary scene, exemplified here in a courtier, and realizing that its decay is over-laid with a glossy veneer. It is this ability of Torres to catch the greater ambience of what he is describing so succinctly and bring home his point so neatly and so chillingly that makes him such an accomplished poet of his day. He is an astute observer of the world about him and reports it as he sees it. In essence he is greatly disillu-sioned with this world and his ability to make this world real to us is realized through his linguistic exaggerations. By deforming this world into a grotesque reflection of what it really is, he makes it more lifelike. We understand, sometimes with difficulty, the mean-ing of what he is saying. It comes to us like the deformed reality of the painting of a Picasso or a Dali. The very deformation hammers this reality itself into our consciousness with relentless insistence. The baroque ambience continues on quite well, then, in Torres. His horror at his world, his disillusion, and the resulting poignance of his work move us deeply. While we may at times be repelled by the disagreeable images and the difficult syntax, we react profoundly to the feeling beneath the words. Because he so well captures this essence of baroque poetry, we may consider Torres the best illustra-tor of baroque or traditionalist poetry in eighteenth-century Spain.

II *The Neoclassic Reaction to "Decadence"*

The neoclassicists as a group did not really promote any active reform until about the middle of the century. Prior to this time of course we have Luzán's *Poetics* which was written for both poetry and the theater. This work, as we saw in the previous chapter, gave guidelines and rules for writing. As in the case of the theater it was some time before they had any effect on those literary genres they sought to renovate. In essence Luzán wished poetry to be clear, to have a message, and to state it succinctly. When we speak of neo-classicism in poetry, as in the theater, we are really referring to reason or rationalism in literature. This rationalism was the basis for the Enlightenment itself; so then we actually are talking of limitation as opposed to exaggeration in form and message. This cardinal precept pertains to all European literatures during this time. Luzán, who establishes this attitude of reason or limit, is essentially talking of good taste. Excess, unnecessary ornamentation, flamboyance are to be abhorred. Unfortunately, such a philosophy naturally leads to a limit on personal expression. The lack of intimacy is probably the source of most criticism leveled against the neoclassicists. In some ways such criticism is just, but it is also to forget the basic tenets of the movement and to apply our own or at least later criteria in our judgments, which perhaps is not fair. For this reason, for example, the criticism that is at times still leveled at Tomás de Iriarte for the apparent coldness of his writing is not at all justified. He himself was a very sensitive person, but because of the dictates of his literary philosophy this sensitivity was relegated to a secondary position in his creative processes.

Neoclassicism in Spanish literature takes a different turn from what it does in other countries such as France. In this latter country it was classical antiquity that mainly provided neoclassic writers their themes and settings. In Spain literary artists looked back to their own national heritage for inspiration, a phenomenon that we have already noted. Their interest in the Renaissance poetry of Garcilaso, Fray Luis, and others is thus easily explained. The influence of those Renaissance writers is great. In fact the example set by those earlier poets provided the standard for neoclassic writing in the 1700s as much as did Luzán's *Poetics*. Two things come to mind at this point. The influence of the Renaissance poets was very much responsible for the reestablishment in the eighteenth century of the old poetic schools — the Sevillian and the Salamancan. The other thing is even more important. It is often asserted, even by critics who should know better, that the French and their contemporary influence were responsible for much of the new direction toward precision and conciseness in Spanish poetry. This is not true. It was rather the nationalistic fervor of the neoclassicists and Luzán's book of rules.

Among the first neoclassic poets the most important was Nicolás Fernández de Moratín, the playwright whose efforts to establish a neoclassic reformation in the theater we have noticed in the previous chapter. Just as he was not the only early writer of tragedies, he was not the only poet in these years, but he nevertheless was the most outstanding for various reasons. One was his bringing together a group of writers with similar interests, the group to be known as the Tertulia de la Fonda de San Sebastián. Among the Tertulia's members were such writers as Ignacio López de Ayala, José Cadalso, Vicente de los Ríos, and Tomás de Iriarte. The interests of the Tertulia were almost totally literary, and naturally it associated itself with change in literary style. The group, led by Moratín, actively sought to impose new rules on the writing of poetry and drama, rules that were expounded by Luzán. Their creative works often were not so important as their critical essays putting forth their viewpoints concerning reform in a clear, precise language. Such was the value of the prefaces to Moratín's tragedies that we mentioned in chapter 3.

Moratín grew up in pleasant surroundings. He was born in 1737 to the wife of a jeweler to Queen Isabel Farnesio. When her husband Philip V died she went to the country palace of La Granja. It was there that Moratín received his first real education. The protection that he enjoyed from the crown in his youth was obviously quite valuable to him in his literary career, for it gave him ready introduction to writers of other countries such as France and Italy. He became a member of the Academy of the Arcadians of Rome under the literary name of Flumisbo Thermodonciaco. Eventually he became a teacher of poetics in the Colegio de San Isidro, a position he at first lost to López de Ayala but which he recovered when the latter became ill. Moratín died in 1780.

His dramatic career was important especially for his ideas for innovation and criticism, as we have already indicated, and this even though his neoclassical tragedies as a whole are probably the best in the Spanish eighteenth century. His poetry is more valuable as a creative production, however. The variety of form is wide — anacreontics, sonnets, odes, etc. There is a shadow of French influence but the overwhelming feeling is Spanish, especially seen in one poem called "Fiesta de toros en Madrid" ("Bullfight in Madrid"). The nationalistic, patriotic fervor of the Spanish neoclassicists is thus once more underscored.

The "Bullfight in Madrid" is essentially a rather overblown description of a bullfight in the time of the Cid. Even though there is a distortion of chronology in the poem, it is valuable for several reasons. First, it demonstrates the ability of the neoclassicists to portray color and ambience. The vitality of the bulls, the awesome power they exhibit at every turn, the ferocity of the Moors who are holding the festival, the seductiveness and artfulness of their women, the innocent meekness of the captive Christian lady (Jimena), and the stalwart strength of the Christian knight (Ruy Díaz, the Cid) are all here. In these attributes the poem is not so completely different from Golden-Age versions of events in the Cid's life. The fictional elements are, nevertheless, much heightened by Moratín, and one feels that he is not so much depicting a supposed event in the Cid's life as he is capturing the flavor of an earlier time in Spanish history.

The next value of the poem is an admirable neoclassic characteristic, the interest in precise detail. Such detail, which anticipates the emphasis on minutiae by the nineteenth-century realists, is nicely seen in two strophes midway through the poem in a description of the bull when confronted by the Cid:

> Offended, the bull paws the sand,
> throwing it over his shoulders,
> twisting his great neck;
> he smells the earth and wets it
> with his hot breathing.
>   He swishes his tail violently,
> whipping his right ear,
> drawing back somewhat,
> so that his strength will be
> greater and his thrust more violent.[6]

The last characteristic of the poem that we shall note is its use of suspense and ominous foreboding, a characteristic that the romantics of the nineteenth century cultivate quite openly. One has only to think of some of the poems and plays of the duke of Rivas. The creation of suspense is noted in several places in Moratín's poem but nowhere so well as in the final strophes when the Moorish mayor and the Cid leave the scene, each hiding his true feelings:

> The mayor, desirous
> of the advantage in Madrid,
> dissimulates a calmness
> and through the flowery park
> goes out with him [the Cid] reasoning.
>   And it is well known that
> the Cid swore before the cross
> of his conquering sword
> not to remove his helmet
> until he should control Madrid.[7]

The sensation of ominous foreboding with which the poem ends is not a characteristic to be seen only in later Spanish literature. It is also very much a medieval one, recalling the oral tradition of the ballads whose story lines could be continued and discontinued depending on the whim of the individual narrator. Very subtly, then, Moratín has recaptured a significant aspect of that national literature which he is striving to both emulate and preserve in his poem.

There are other writers who belong to this first phase of neo-classic reformation of poetry. None of them has the stature of the elder Moratín, but two deserve mention here. The first is José María Vaca de Guzmán, who is principally remembered today for having defeated both Moratín father and Moratín son in literary competitions in the late 1770s and early 1780s. These were established by the Royal Academy to encourage more serious interest in the writing of literature. The contests themselves were important not so much for the works that were produced for them as for the fact that they called for material commemorating events of national glory and renown. As previously observed, this emphasis on Spain's glorious past is a part of that revival of interest in events and figures of the Golden Age and medieval period. In the first competition in 1777 the subject proposed for prose was a eulogy of Philip V, the intention being to praise the king responsible for the founding of the academy. The theme for poetry was Cortés' destruction of his ships before entering Mexico in 1519. This theme was felt to be superlatively heroic. Forty-five compositions were presented in the poetry division. Men of recognized literary reputation participated, but the prize (presented on August 13, 1778) went to the then unknown (and still so today) poet Vaca de Guzmán. In the competition in 1778 Vaca was again victorious. Moratín the younger, aged nineteen at the time, won the second prize. The competition of 1780 drew many participants, and the prize went to Juan Meléndez Valdés, then virtually unknown, for his bucolic poem entitled "Batilo."

Vaca de Guzmán is of little real importance except that he does illustrate excellently the successful attempts of many poets to write better and to achieve national recognition for their efforts. He was born in 1744 and was well educated in his youth. He led a very active life, yet found the time and the inclination to change the existing situation in the production of poetry. He is representative of so many others who sought change, were successful in their short-lived attempts, and who have been forgotten because of the Moratíns and the Meléndez Valdés', who were of course much greater writers. The efforts of people such as Guzmán should not be overlooked, however.

The other writer we mention here in this section is Juan José López de Sedano, mentioned in chapter 3. He was born in 1730 and died in 1801. His literary and other activities were varied and his best claim to fame is probably his tragedy *Jahel* (1763). He belongs to the first group of neoclassic dramatists headed by Moratín the elder. But we are mainly concerned with him now because of his nine-volume anthology published between 1768 and 1778: *Parnaso español. Colección de poesías escogidas de los más célebres poetas castellanos* (*Spanish Parnassus. Collection of Poems Selected From the Most Famous Spanish Poets*). The idea of the work is an excellent one — to make available to the general reading public the most significant literary works of Spain's past. Unfortunately, Sedano was not always judicious in his selections. This failure aroused the enmity of one acerbic critic in particular, Tomás de Iriarte. He attacked Sedano in his *Donde las dan las toman (Give and Take)*. Iriate had indeed been goaded into his attack by Sedano earlier so we must not fault him too severely for his criticism of the anthology's editor. Iriarte's polemical essay caused the cessation of Sedano's labors on the *Parnassus* and no further volumes appeared. We shall not argue here about the necessity of the argument. The *Parnassus* had much value. It did make people more conscious of their literary heritage and herin lies the anthology's significance for us today. It once more illustrates the change in attitude regarding the writing of poetry that had at last begun to take hold in the second half of the century. Whether the efforts of so many people were always completely successful is today unimportant. The fact that they saw a need for change and actively sought to bring it about is very important, however.

III   *The Fabulists*

Probably the most outstanding and lasting contribution of the neoclassicists was the composing of fables. In no other genre was the *utile dulci* of Horace so well demonstrated. In addition, the popularity of these poems has lasted until today. The fables themselves are still included in school texts for children in Spain and elsewhere. No better accolade could be given the fabulists, for they have become established as neoclassic poets par excellence, and, even more notable, they continue to enlighten young minds of the twentieth century.

There are two fabulists who concern us — Félix María de Samaniego and Tomás de Iriarte. Samaniego was born in 1745 and died in 1801. For the most part he lived as a country gentleman, very similar to his ubiquitous English counterpart of the day. He was involved in local matters as well as some of a more national flavor while at the same time managing to remain the convivial host on his country estate.

Samaniego's literary fame rests principally on his *Fábulas morales* (*Moral Fables*) published in 1781. In his prologue he states that he set out to imitate the classical fabulists both ancient and modern: Aesop, Phaedrus, and La Fontaine. His fables are perhaps not so clever and ingenious nor so concise as those of his sources, but he does express himself in a most matter-of-fact and sensible way. The following verses give us a good idea of Samaniego's style and the strongly moralistic intent of his poems:

> A certain craftsman painted
> a battle in which a single
> man, so brave,
> conquered a horrible lion.
> Another lion, which saw the painting,
> without asking about the artist,
> in a deprecating tone
> said: *"One can well see*
> *that painting is an illusion*
> *and that the painter was not a lion."*
> ("The Lion conquered by the Man")[8]

The history of the *Moral Fables* leads us into our discussion of Iriarte. Samaniego finished writing the collection in 1779 and sent it to Iriarte for his comments. This action in itself indicates the esteem in which Iriarte was held at the time. Iriarte's opinion was favorable, and with this reassuring impetus Samaniego sent his poems to press. Ironically, considering what was to happen, the third book was dedicated to Iriarte:

> In my verses, Iriarte,
> I wish no more art
> Than to have yours as a model.
> To compete I desire

With your genius, which the learned world admires,
If you lend me your lyre,
The one on which played sweetly
Music and *Poetry* jointly.[9]

In spite of all this supposedly good feeling between Samaniego and Iriarte, when Iriarte's fables appeared in 1782, Samaniego declared himself on the side of Iriarte's enemies. The reason for this change in attitude must lie in a comment by the editor of Iriarte's fables. The statement is especially innocent when one considers the inherent differences of purpose in the two works. The editor writes: "I do not wish to prejudice the readers' judgment about their merit [of the fables], but only to note to those least versed in our literature that this is the first collection of entirely original fables that has been published in Spanish. And thus as it has for Spain this particular recommendation, it has even another for foreign nations: that is, the novelty of all its themes being related to literature."[10]

This statement, plus the failure to mention Samaniego's name, caused the latter's resultant petulance. His reaction is really quite unacceptable when one considers that Iriarte cites him handsomely in his *Para casos tales suelen tener los maestros oficiales* (*For Just Such Cases Do They Have Trained Teachers*). It is also worth mentioning that Iriarte was a well-known figure while Samaniego was virtually unknown — the fact that Samaniego felt obliged to have Iriarte's approval before publishing the fables is sufficient indication. However unjust we may consider his petulant childishness, he did proceed to publish an anonymous pamphlet, without printer or place indicated, called blatantly enough *Observaciones sobre las Fábulas literarias originales de D. Tomás de Iriarte* (*Observations on the "Original" Literary Fables of Tomás de Iriarte*). The pamphlet was not sold but was sent to the more renowned members of court society.

This tactic sounds all too much like the devious ways employed both before and after by Iriarte's other, more damaging enemy Juan Pablo Forner. Samaniego, while wanting us to believe he is an impartial critic, succeeds in condemning the whole concept of the suitability of the fable to provide rules concerning the production of literary works. We might ask at this point how it is that animals are that much better suited to teach morals — the normal purpose of the fable and of Samaniego's own collection — than they are to inculcate literary precepts. Samaniego's censure becomes both ridiculous and ludicrous when we carry his assertions to a logical conclusion.

Fortunately, Iriarte made no reply to Samaniego in print, but he did attempt to have legal action brought against him, since the pamphlet had appeared without the necessary license of authority. Nothing came of this action, except the discovery of Forner's work *Los gramáticos: historia chinesca (The Grammarians: A Chinese History)*. Forner was seeking to have his work published under his real name, which he had not done previously in his quarrel with Iriarte, but the Iriartes were successful in keeping it from going to press.

The *Literary Fables,* published in 1782, caused quite an uproar when they appeared. This book, which gave Iriarte his most lasting fame, represents the quintessence of his ideas concerning literature, being actually a synthesis of the motivations behind his previous works and those that would follow. The collection contains a motto that pertains to all Iriarte's works: "Usus vetusto genere, sed rebus novis" ("The use of an old genre but with new aims"). Emilio Cotarelo y Mori has some very good comments concerning this motto and what it implies:

Iriarte's genius, looking for a field in which to spread its wings and not finding it in the known literary forms, decided to create new genres, or even among the common ones to move along unexplored paths, with the purpose of freeing itself if only in part from those precepts obtained through formal education which imprisoned and sterilized his imagination, so fresh and rich as few were among the writers of his time. Thus was born the dialogue *Give and Take,* a polemical work, new in form and agreeable and instructive reading; thus the poem *Music,* which he took up after convincing himself that no one had preceded him in a similar undertaking; and thus he produced his celebrated *Literary Fables.*[11]

The purpose of Iriarte's writing the fables was to set up a body of literary precepts or guidelines for writing — and to point out the most common defects in contemporary works. His ideas are hardly new and neither are they unduly profound. Their value lies rather in their being a convenient source of reference for the incipient writer. The style of the collection, in addition to its following the precepts herein set forth, is pleasant: Iriarte is carrying out, albeit obviously, at least painlessly, the *utile dulci.* The Frenchman Vézinet gives a concise idea of the *Fables:* "The *Literary Fables* form a critique of poetry; they also form a collection of satires and, at the time, personal satires at that. An ardent polemicist, Iriarte relentlessly berates those who do not adopt the doctrines of our classicists. Against affectation, against pomposity, against extravagance, against confusion, he leads in Spain the combat that Boileau led in France a century earlier. Like Boileau he is an alert and hard censor for all 'penholders'.''[12]

In another place Vézinet succinctly defines Iriarte's real contribution to Spanish literature. "The superiority of Iriarte?" he writes: "It rests above all in his invention. He imagines and then invents his subjects."[13] Iriarte's "inventiveness" is most visible in the selection of the genre of the fable to expound his views. The fable is of itself naturally didactic and yet it can be among the most entertaining of all types of literature. In the mere choice of vehicle we see that Iriarte is following his guide, Horace, whose work he had translated only five years earlier.

Ever since the publication of the *Literary Fables* it has been the subject of much discussion because of the allusions it supposedly contained to contemporary figures. In fact, it was these supposed allusions that caused so many of the early polemics. The value of the poems, however, does not lie in their providing some sort of guessing game. To dwell on the question of allusion is to meander through a maze trod by critics for nearly two hundred years. Yet we must admit that the subject is pertinent in one major way. It is this aspect of the work that caused it to gain much of its initial popularity and pushed Iriarte's name even higher in literary circles. The possibility of slander or mere gossip is always enough to entice a waiting and willing audience.

The restoration of order and symmetry in language especially and in the arts and in life generally is Iriarte's basic purpose then. While the fables treat a variety of subjects, Iriarte follows four essential themes that expound on this purpose: (1) style, (2) the traditionalists versus the moderns, (3) the mentality of the mass man, and (4) the meaning of criticism.

Fable 5, "The Two Parrots and the Magpie," illustrates an aspect of Iriarte's concern with style. It is a question noted with and after Feijoo — the "Frenchifying" of the Spanish language. In the fable one parrot is French, another Spanish. The latter imitates the former in all respects until one day he finally emits some mongrel French. A magpie laughs at him, which elicits a haughty, pompous reply: " 'You are nothing but a purist, / Of taste foolishly exclusive.' / 'Thanks for the compliment,' quoth Magpie, curtly.''[14] The concept of *purist* is not bad therefore, when it stands in sharp contrast to ignorance. The subtlety of Iriarte is immediately noticeable. The way in which he manages to maintain a straight line between the pro- and anti-Gaulists is striking. He elaborates on this theme in *For Just Such Cases:* "Add to this that just as those antipurists against whom you [Iriarte] so correctly direct the fable of 'The Two Parrots and the Magpie' unnecessarily introduce words and, what is worse, foreign phrases doing irreparable damage to our language because they deem it so poor as to need to be dressed in foreign finery, so do they offend it who, at the opposite extreme, renew long-forgotten terms with no urgent motive, supposing it [the language] so poor as to need to take up again its once discarded finery."[15]

The war between the traditionalists and the moderns receives its first treatment in fable 4, "The Drones and the Bee." The tone is muted, but the title amply indicates the disparaging attitude of the writer toward those who only imitate and do not create. It is this sterile characteristic of the worst traditionalists that Iriarte always condemned. Here the fabulist is taking aim at those who refuse to admit invention and decry all newness, preferring to hide because of their own inferiority in the shadow of acceptable works produced much earlier: "How many there are, who their emptiness mask, / By quoting wise words from the lips of the dead! / But with all their pretence, did they ever, I ask, / Produce any such from their own shallow head?"[16]

In another poem he more directly reprimands those who forsake their own literature for those foreign letters considered fashionable at the moment; Iriarte again follows a middle road in his attack. This particular fable (16), "The Tea Plant and Sage," deals with two plants often more appreciated by foreign nations than by their own. The sage says to the tea plant:

> "Good luck attend you to my native shore!
> For never yet was any nation known,
> But gold and praises will profusely pour
> On foreign products, while it slights its own."
> Now, I am sure that I can Spaniards show,
> Who will eternally be quoting
> Whole pages out of Tasso or Boileau;
> Yet never think or care to know
> What languages Garcilaso wrote in.[17]

As for the "mass man," Iriarte is not really concerned with him as a societal or cultural entity. Yet on several occasions he ventures criticisms of the *taste* of the mass man — that is, a taste that is indiscriminate, easily swayed or perverted, and lacking in aesthetic authority. As a result of this concept he declares himself against the idea of caprice or whim so characteristic of this type of person. We cannot say that Iriarte is openly antidemocratic in his views of the common man. What he does feel and express agrees completely with his inherent belief in the necessity for authority and order. Since this belief is inherent in all really enlightened people of the time, no matter how much they may have glorified the idea of freedom and individuality, it is not surprising to find it here in the *Literary Fables*. Beneath Iriarte's diatribes against the tastes of the mass man, there is still a respect for the man who remains true to himself and does not bow to the dictates of a senseless authority.

The result of the mentality criticized in this group of fables is the subject of number 17, "The Linnet and the Swan." The swan's song is boasted of grandly, but when put to the test it is only a grotesque cackle: "Not strange, that empty reputation, / Without, or skill or genius, at foundation, / Should, upon trial, cheat the expectation!"[18] Much needless folly would cease in the area of letters if the mentality of the mass man were no longer heeded. Such is the message of Fable 32, "The Fop and the Lady":

> A famous gallant, of Parisian renown . . .
> On the festival day of his lady love placed
> On his shoes two paltry buckles of tin;
> In order to show, by this frivolous whim,
> That he courted not fame, but that fame courted him.
> "What beautiful silver, so brilliant and gay!"
> Said the lady. "Huzza for the taste and the rule
> Of the master of fashion, the pride of our day!"
>
> Thus a volume of nonsense, or, I am a fool,
> The world will devour, if subscribed with the name
> Of a popular author, established in fame.[19]

The meaning and the purpose of criticism are the last general subject of the fables. The frustration and anger Iriarte felt at the hands of unjust and envious critics undoubtedly had much to do with the subject matter and tone of the poems in this grouping. Iriarte states very simply in fable 34 that envy and jealousy are often the foundations of criticism: "When envious detractors find / In wise men's works, no welcome faults, / They satisfy their spiteful mind / By base and personal assaults."[20] Obviously reacting to the type of criticism that had been openly directed against him, Iriarte, having noted what this criticism is, states the dire consequences that come to this type of critic. In fable 30, "The Author and the Rat," a rat keeps eating a scholar's library. Finally the author puts poison in his ink and abruptly ends the rat's career:

> Sarcastic said the Poet, thus relieved:
> "Let him, who gnaws too freely, have a care
> Lest his malicious insult prove a snare;
> And the impatient wight he seeks to bait,
> Should write him in corrosive sublimate."[21]

At the other extreme, Iriarte says that criticism should not be used as a vehicle to applaud a work unnecessarily. To promote this end is to pervert criticism as surely as to use it out of personal vindictiveness. Fable 57, "The Lizards," deals with the harm resulting from lavishing too much attention on very insignificant objects:

> It is not worth the while to flatter
> The pride of writers we despise.
> 'Tis honoring too much the matter,
> To condescend to criticize.
> Their paltry trash in serious way
> To note — your pains will never pay.[22]

The diffusion of the *Literary Fables* has been notable. The editions in Spanish since 1782 have been numerous, and they continue to be printed well into the present century. The translations have been equally remarkable and show the immediate popularity the poems gained outside Spain. The first translation was into Portuguese in 1796; an English translation appeared in 1804. Some mention should be made too of early advances in American letters — Devereux's translation (the one I have used here) was published in Boston in 1855. Interestingly, it appears not long after Ticknor's landmark work on Spanish literature.

The *Literary Fables* are definitely unique in Spanish literature. They are the only Spanish art of poetry that really does "please while teaching." If such were not the case, the *Fables* would hardly have retained their popularity. In addition to this more literary aspect of their value, they have a personal importance for Iriarte.

They are the culmination of his literary career although they appear some nine years before his death. They come as a natural result of the teachings imbibed in his youth and show in him that genius of originality that he always preached. The combination of originality and adherence to rules is nowhere else so evident or so fruitful in Spanish literature. By delineating so well the poet's tenets and even his own personal idiosyncrasies, the *Fables* should be considered one of the most significant works of the neoclassic spirit in the Spanish eighteenth century.

IV   *Rise of a New Literary Mentality*

One of the most strange and fascinating phenomena of eighteenth-century Spanish literature is the existence of various philosophical and aesthetic outlooks that develop and overlap often at the same time. We have seen how the baroque or traditionalist mentality endures throughout the century. Whether it is fought by a Feijoo, Luzán, Moratín, or Iriarte, it is always there raising its frustrating head to the enlightened and neoclassic messiahs. When these latter do eventually succeed in their various fields, there is still the further frustration, especially in poetry, of a new outlook. This new outlook, attitude, or mentality is very important in our discussion, for it eventually develops into the full-blown (or one might say, overblown) romanticism of the early nineteenth century. Until the last twenty years or so very few critics would even consider that Spanish romanticism existed before the likes of an Espronceda, Larra, or the duke of Rivas. With one notable exception before roughly 1960, no one was willing to admit that Spanish romanticism had a long history, from approximately 1770 on. This exception was the marvelous twentieth-century romantic, Azorín:

From time to time one thinks about the origins of Spanish romanticism. They have been recently discussed because of the intention to found a museum of romanticism. What are the origins of romanticism in Spain? From what basis can we find such an esthetic movement springing? And what precursors shall we assign to the systematically declared romantics? The romantic movement in Spain and in France has roots deep in the eighteenth century. In France those antecedents have been carefully studied, but in Spain ... they have not been studied yet.... There is one author who has carried out in Spain Chateaubriand's mission in France.... We are alluding to Meléndez Valdés. How is it that when speaking of the romantic movement in Spain Meléndez Valdés is never cited? All of romanticism is already contained — impetuous and fiery — in Meléndez. In him we find the pronounced subjectivism of the romantic: the melancholy, the solemn emphasis, the unevenness between idea and expression, the taste for horrible spectacles, the tenderness, the tears, and the infinite despair.[23]

Since about 1960 it has been critics like Russell P. Sebold in this country who have sought to give more perspective to our view of Spanish romanticism. It is to critics like him that we are indebted for a comprehension of romanticism in Spain as a cohesive, cosmopolitan, long-lived development, and not something that suddenly sprang forth in the 1830s. This new interpretation, certainly a needed and sane one, continues the ideas of Azorín just noted and of others ideas of his as well: "A great sentimental revolution was being announced. The eighteenth century criticized everything: emotions, ideas, institutions. Everything was belittled, pulverized, and destroyed. Actually the only thing that remained sublime was the personality of the critic; that is, the 'I' that considers and examines everything. . . . Meléndez arrives at this moment of universal disintegration. . . . The poet finds himself all alone, despairing, agonizing at the ruins of all old beliefs and feelings. What can he lean on? What does the future hold in store for him? To whom can he turn?"[24]

Azorín goes on to say that everything found in the romanticism of the nineteenth century is in Meléndez. The only thing not really visible is a sense of the picturesque, the return to the Middle Ages for inspiration, and the taste for the archaic: "And that is the only way in which later romantics — Zorrilla, Rivas, García Gutiérrez — have surpassed him. Meléndez brought everything else to art: lyrical exaltation, shattering melancholy, and the richness and profusion of a dictionary."[25]

With such new interpretations and criticisms of the founder of romanticism in Spain, we must look at his background. In this way we shall see the early development of that literary movement, which in Spain has certain facets that antecede their counterparts in the rest of Europe. Meléndez Valdés was born in 1754. His mother died some seven years later and her death had a great effect on his early literary career. He was an introspective, sensitive poet in his first years and undoubtedly the breakup of his family had much to do with creating his personality. Meléndez suffered further familial disruptions at a relatively young age, and these too added to his sympathetic understanding of life and also increased his desire to escape from a reality that often seemed very pressing. He was educated in Madrid and at the University of Salamanca, which became for him a sort of refuge throughout later, more troubled times. In 1773 he became a friend of Cadalso, whose friendship would have important influence on his budding literary career. A year later his father died, and in 1777 his brother Esteban, who had acted as a sort of parent, died. These traumas turned Meléndez more and more to his friends. These, especially Cadalso and Jovellanos, would guide him much as older brothers and teachers.

The most significant event of his literary career came at the beginning with his winning first prize in the Royal Academy's literary competition in 1780 for his eclogue "Batilo." In 1782 he married a woman several years older than himself. María Andrea de Coca was the kind of wife Meléndez needed — regimented, demanding, motherly, and yet very loving. Following their marriage Meléndez' received the doctor-of-law degree in 1783. In 1785 Meléndez' first volume of poetry was published to immediate and wide acclaim. But not long after this he chose that other love of his life — law. In 1789 he was notified of his nomination as a magistrate in the criminal court at Zaragoza. In the next eight years he held several legal posts and by 1797 had been appointed district attorney of Madrid. Interestingly, his literary pursuits had not ended, for in this same year a three-volume edition of his works was published. The following year he was elected to the Royal Academy. For the next several years he was in and out of favor with the government as the winds of change, emanating from France in this turbulent period, affected his legal career. Between 1802 and 1808 he stayed in Salamanca, where for the most part he had peace from the turmoil encountered earlier in Madrid. In the spring of 1808 he returned to Madrid and was almost immediately sent to Asturias by the Junta Central to report back on recent public disorders there. He was nearly killed by a mob that was not too pleased with any investigation whatever from the government in Madrid. After involvement in the Bonaparte government, Meléndez went into exile in France in 1813 with the fall of that government. In 1817 he died in Montpellier, still longing to return to his homeland.

To consider Meléndez' literary activities we must first look at his membership in a school of poets at the University of Salamanca when he was a student there. This group would later be called the

Salamancan School of Poetry. This title is a direct linkage to the more famous sixteenth-century group of poets known by the same name. The nucleus of eighteenth-century poets at Salamanca held sway as arbiters of poetic taste in the 1770s and 1780s. Forming the core of this eighteenth-century Salamancan School of Poets were three students and three Augustine clerics, of the same order as the leader of the sixteenth-century school, Fray Luis de León. The three clerics were Diego Tadeo González (Delio), Juan Fernández de Rojas (Liseno), and Andrés del Corral (Andrenio). The students were José Iglesias de la Casa (Arcadio), Juan Pablo Forner (Amintas), and Meléndez Valdés (Batilo). Forner's nature was too polemical to allow him to remain a member of the group for long. Nicasio Álvarez de Cienfuegos and Manuel José Quintana are also considered members of the group although they were much younger than the others.

Cadalso served as the solidifier of the group when he came to Salamanca in 1773. The poets he encountered were following the tenets of the neoclassic school with its dual emphasis on utility and pleasure. Like the Spanish neoclassic writers in general, they looked for inspiration in outstanding writers of Spain's Golden Age. The influence of the sixteenth-century writers, especially Garcilaso and Fray Luis de León, was therefore just as important as that of Horace. The members of the Salamancan School did not always exhibit a certain formality seen at times in some neoclassic poets. They did not necessarily reject any aims of the neoclassicists, but rather amplified them to include currently developing attitudes and philosophies. Their poetry is thus quite diverse in form and outlook: tender, bucolic, sensual, melancholy, sentimental, philosophical, social, and at times even political.

Diego González, the unofficial leader of the group, was born in 1733 and quite early saw in Fray Luis his model for writing poetry. He began to write *liras,* the poetic form introduced into Spain by Garcilaso and then perfected by Fray Luis in the second half of the sixteenth century. More important for the development of a poetic style and attitude for himself and his followers was González' emphasis on decorum, simple elegance, and harmony of the subject and its treatment in his poems. These characteristics are particularly evident in Fray Luis' poetry. As we might expect, Meléndez, the direct disciple of both González and of Fray Luis, very nicely evidences them also.

When Cadalso arrived in Salamanca in May, 1773, he was much

taken with the attitude of this small group of poets, an attitude that was so different from the generally repressive one of the university as a whole. He was especially impressed with the youthful exuberance and sensitivity of Meléndez, to whom Cadalso's travels and resultant sophistication were attractive. The appeal of a new and foreign world with its different outlooks and philosophies almost immediately began to take hold in Meléndez' mind. Changes in his outlook began to appear so that what might have been at first a purely neoclassic attitude became more open and less unyielding. We may say that an incipient "romantic" attitude manifests itself from a very early point in his literary career. From his first days as a poet to his death, we find him following a dual path in his writing of poetry. A classical point of view is exhibited in his imitation of Horace, in the writing itself of anacreontics, and in the use of classical metrical forms such as the ode. Yet within this very writing, he expresses very personal themes and he begins to include new eighteenth-century philosophies in the anacreontics themselves. And at the same time he is searching for old and different classical meters, he looks for purely Spanish ones to enrich his poetic expression. His eventual, almost excessive cultivation of the *romance* is a good example.

Ignacio de Luzán held that pleasure was principally an intellectual one since it was derived from studying models, themselves based on nature. With this search for models, particularly from the 1500s, went a revival of interest in the pastoral mode of that time, a mode in itself an imitation of an antique genre. This revived interest, in an elementary but blatant way, is seen in the use of Arcadian names by the Salamancan poets. It is moreover a good indication of the poets' inherent desire for a renovation of poetic expression. Even more important is that, in itself, the use of Arcadian names emphasizes the poets' insistence on a personal touch and a closeness with nature which set them off from the other, more formal neoclassicists. The more immediate longing for nature, for physical contact with her, eventually carried the school beyond the tenets of Luzán and pure Spanish neoclassicism.

During the 1770s Meléndez thus began to withdraw from a total commitment to neoclassical precepts. Luzán's formulas, to be sure, were still active in guiding his creative abilities, but they were subjected to a secondary position. The innate sensitivity of the poet's personality became responsible for a more intimate, personal outlook. It is at this point that he can best be compared to Tomás de

Iriarte, who so well represents the Spanish neoclassicist of the times. Iriarte had feelings, naturally, but his aesthetic criteria would not permit him to express them openly. Meléndez, had he possessed the desire for control that Iriarte possessed, would have been little different from his contemporary. But Meléndez, because of his inherently sensitive nature and his readings of English and French writers, set forth on a divergent path from Iriarte's. Meléndez eventually affirmed that the best form of artistic expression is that which communicates the artist's emotion directly to other men. Such expression meant the denuding of himself in his verses and ultimately made him vulnerable to both love and attack from his fellowman.

Meléndez left a huge amount of poetry written throughout his life. Some of it is airy and light in tone, and for many years critics tended to say that all his poetry is that way. Such is not the case, of course, and even those poems that are indeed superficially frivolous have an underlying pathos beneath their happy surface. In the various editions the beginning poems are designated as "Odas anacreónticas" ("Anacreontic Odes"). There are only twenty-four of them in the 1785 edition, whereas their number is greatly increased in later publications. The mood of anacreontic poetry was well suited to Meléndez' purposes as reiterated in the first poem of the 1785 and later editions:

> Not with my peaceful lyre
> In sad laments
> Will the fortunes be sung
> Of unhappy kings;
> Nor the cry of the soldier
> Fierce in battle
> Nor the thunder with which
> The horrible bronze spits forth its ball.
> I tremble and shudder;
> For inspiration does not permit
> Tender lips
> Such sublime songs.
> I am a youth, and I want
> To say more pleasant things
> And delight myself
> With dances and parties.[26]

This type of poetry — gentle or boisterous in tone and varied in form — celebrates the love between two people. Sometimes, however, the love that the poetry depicts is not reciprocated and, as a result, the poet is provided the opportunity to bewail his desolate fate. Still, whether the poet has been fortunate or not in his love affairs, when he is declaiming his feelings for the beloved, he expresses himself with great exuberance. Meléndez expresses both the positive and negative attitudes in his verses. His use of the anacreontic is part of that genre's long development throughout Western Europe. In Spain, Meléndez brings this type of poetry to its greatest achievement, not only in style but in popularity with the general Spanish public.

These poems are varied in content and feeling. Whereas one might be flippant like "To My Readers," another might be quite serious. The ballads particularly show this diversity. One of the most beautiful in expression is number 15, "Los segadores" ("The Harvesters"). The poem is fairly long, beginning and ending with the same four-line stanza. The regularity of the meter enhances the settled, calm ambience. The scene begs comparison to the early nineteenth-century painting *The Cornfield* by the English artist John Constable. The same fragile, ethereal beauty that that painting evokes is here in Meléndez' poem. In essence, the poem is a praise of country life personalized in an old man who talks of nature and of God who has put order in His universe for the good of all creatures.

There are other divisions of Meléndez' poetry — *sonetos, silvas, elegías, epístolas, discursos,* etc. They all contain evidences of the so-called lighter vein of his thought as well as more profoundly philosophical and political expression. Contrary to some critics' affirmations, we must emphasize that it is impossible to divide his poetry conveniently into two categories — one, light poetry that abruptly becomes a second more philosophical outpouring after Jovellanos' influence on Meléndez is stronger in the late 1770s and early 1780s. Meléndez' attitudes cover a wide spectrum, from high effervescence to deep melancholy. The whole group of sonnets reminds us of this fact at once. The variety of emotions achieved by the poet in this rigid form is astonishing. The effusive tone of his poetry is more akin to that of rococo art. Just as such art is not really superficial, neither is this type of Meléndez' poetry. Also, just as painting in the eighteenth century is quite varied, so are Meléndez' early poems. In his first years Meléndez followed essentially rococo dictates. Even more important, tones of that school permeate all his poetry, mingling with new romantic inspirations.

Actually, before the appearance of Luzán's *Poetics* in 1737, the art of poetry had undergone vast changes, principally in the direction of more individuality on the part of the writer. This gradual change had been occurring ever since the appearance of Francis Bacon's inductive philosophy in the early seventeenth century. Somewhat later the concept of personal observation inherent in this philosophy was joined to the concept of experience of Sir Isaac Newton's empirical physics. At the very end of the seventeenth century, John Locke expounded his sensationalist doctrine, maintaining that all our knowledge originates in sensation or sense perceptions or, more precisely still, that all man's knowledge is made up of sense elements. In the eighteenth century Condillac applied Locke's philosophy to the interpretation of poetry. Sensationalism, to use one word to designate this philosophical current, was at the heart of this gradual development of poetics.

The relationship of man and nature in Meléndez' poetry is one wherein nature is innocent and pure, acting as a sort of refuge for man in his escape from the real world of everyday life. The idea sounds not unlike that of the *beatus ille* (Blessed is he), yet in Meléndez' new outlook man becomes at times an almost pitiable creature who looks for succor from a kind of maternal being. There were other writers who expressed this literary viewpoint and who conceivably influenced Meléndez. Principal among these were James Thomson with his *Seasons* (1726–1730) and the marquis of Saint-Lambert with his *Les Saisons* (*The Seasons*) (1769).

The powerful destruction of which nature is capable comes out forcefully in ode 16, "La noche de invierno" ("Winter Night"). The poet's attraction to this power is very striking. The influence of Thomson, at times evident in the subject and wording, is also seen in the hypnotic rapture that overtakes the poet as he is released this time from the tranquillity of self into the fury of nature around him. The important thing is that he is carried away from himself into an isolation that only he can experience. Nature has reached into his most inner being and brought out from his subconscious all the frustrations and anger he feels within. Nature's ability to provide purgation, refuge, and consolation is, of course, at the basis of the concept of nature as a universal mirror.

The importance of solitude and night, as parts of nature, stands out very well in ode 11, "La noche y la soledad" ("Night and Solitude"), written in 1779. Nature is at a further stage of development in the poet's mind in this instance and reflects not so much Thomson or Saint-Lambert as Edward Young in his *Night Thoughts*. There may very well be, too, an influence from Cadalso's *Noches lúgubres* (*Lugubrious Nights*). In his poem Meléndez seeks out the solitude nature provides. The somewhat sepulchral tone is significant here and recalls Young, whom Meléndez cites by name. The consoling effect of solitude is emphasized when it calms a troubled heart. At one point the *beatus-ille* theme joins with another so typical of the eighteenth century — that of virtue. It is not surprising to come upon the theme of friendship further on in the poem, since it was considered the principal means of achieving virtue among the Salamancan poets. The poem is dedicated to Jovellanos, and it is to him Meléndez speaks in words greatly reminiscent of Fray Luis de León in the following verses:

> When will come the day, bright and pure,
> That in gentle solitude joined with you
> My anxious soul
> Can dry its tears,
> Where free in the most solitary and hidden forest
> And at the foot of the most leafy tree,
> In celestial repose
> May we contemplate such sublime truths?
> Hasten, oh heavens!, such days,
> And let us play the funereal cither,
> Oh, Young, that you played....[27]

The idea of the above lines is emphasized in the last verses of the poem where a sort of ethereal peace is achieved. Solitude draws the poet and Jovellanos to nature's bosom. The inherent sadness and melancholy are once more stressed by the reference to Young. Nature does more here than merely reflect the poet's inner longings for peace. Through his projection of himself and his friend on to nature, he makes nature his own, his very self. This kind of interaction between man and nature is what Locke had in mind. Meléndez addresses Jovellanos in these words:

> You, gentle friend, who know the value
> Of meditation, and how much the soul
> Gains through solitude,
> Come....
> And with Young let us silently enter
> In soft peace those lovely places,

Where in their sublime nights let us meditate
A thousand divine truths,
And moved by their lamenting voices,
Let us repeat their lugubrious moans.[28]

From here Meléndez goes further in his developing relation of poet and nature and introduces the most important of all romantic theories — that of *mal du siècle* or, as we should call it now, at least regarding Spanish literature, *fastidio universal*. To see how Meléndez develops this theory and with it further brings about the birth of Spanish romanticism, we shall look at several more poems. We must emphasize the inherent tenderness Meléndez exhibits in his poetry. Many critics have used his sensitivity as a basis for asserting that he was a weak man. We can convincingly argue, however, that such statements are not at all founded in real fact. This tenderness of Meléndez is principally what allowed him to escape the neo-classic aesthetic and receive new philosophical waves that had developed in his century. Ode 33, "Que no son flaqueza la ternura y el llanto" ("Tenderness and Tears Are Not Weakness") is a declaration of the necessity for the poet's own particular creative attitude and a strong defense of his sensitive, lachrymose side. The love Meléndez had for his fellowman, his humanitarianism, is also notable in the verses below:

Do you marvel that I cry;
That my gentle breast
Breaks forth in a rain of tears,
And so fervently implores Heaven?
Not an effeminate weakness
Nor a dull cowardliness
Are the cause of my crying; for my soul
Knows how to suffer with strict constancy....
Everywhere I look
In eternal suffering
I find man moaning; from my compassion
My tears are born, and because of his pain I sigh....[29]

These sentiments lead naturally into those of one of Meléndez' most popular poems, ode 24, "A la mañana, en mi desamparo y orfandad" ("To Morning, on my Abandonment and Orphanhood"). The structure of the piece is, first of all, interesting. The poem is divided into approximately two equal parts. The first contains one of Meléndez' most beautiful descriptions of morning. The second part is a description of the poet in despair. The beauty of morning is bluntly contrasted with his own feelings of desolation. A poem by the duke of Rivas, "El faro de Malta" ("The Lighthouse of Malta"), is greatly reminiscent in its structure of that of Meléndez' poem. The basic sentiments are not too different either, although the nineteenth-century poet feels abandoned because of political exile from Spain. Meléndez' reason is more a familial, personal one — the death of his brother. The description of nature is exquisite:

> In nacre clouds morning,
> Watering the withered earth with pearls,
> Approaches from the east;
> Her cheeks roselike,
> Of a candescent light her transparent veil,
> And much purer than jasmine her face.
> With her whiteness she does not permit
> The sad mantle of opaque night
> Or its squadron of bright stars
> To wrap the earth in blindness and fear;
> But with light steps,
> Spreading her divine and pure light,
> She goes forcing them into the dark west.[30]

The message of the more personal part is what most intrigues us in the poem. Meléndez feels completely alone and has fallen into that pit of total despair toward which he has all along been heading. At his entrance into the abyss he appears somewhat stoic. He is desolated, but stands firm in the following verses:

> I alone, miserable, whom the skies
> Afflict so seriously, with the dawn
> Do not feel happiness,
> But rather more grief....
> Nor can I, oh!, stop my moaning,
> An orphan, young, alone, and helpless.[31]

Meléndez' pose before the universe awaiting some sort of consolation in the last line above clearly reflects the romantic's reshaping of nature in the image of his own psyche. This attitude is very evident in elegy 2, "El melancólico, a Jovino" ("The Melancholy One, to Jovino") in which the term *fastidio universal* first occurs. The date is 1794, long before the terms *mal du siècle* or *Welt-*

schmerz, the more common names for this phenomenon, ever appeared. The importance of the senses is absolute. At this stage of expectant confrontation, nature shares the poet's feelings and eventually merges with him to become one. And here we are at the universalization of the romantic poet's grief. The poet is supreme at last. He is the creator of everything — his view of nature, his mood, and his verses. In so many words, he is definitively the author of his pathetic fallacy. He achieves this ultimate situation through a particular state of mind — through what Meléndez calls *fastidio universal.* In this state, the individual sufferer experiences frustration, despair, and a loss of personal initiative for the positive.

Meléndez' picture of a totally despairing man is precisely what all the Byrons, Mussets, and Esproncedas were to portray in the nineteenth century. As we look at the following lines from Meléndez' elegy, we must remember two very significant things. First, Meléndez provides a term in the Spanish language for an emotional and "artistic" state long before such terms existed in other European languages. (English still does not have such a term.) And, second, Meléndez simply by using the term advances the early development of Spanish romanticism and emphasizes his primary position in that development:

> I see nothing, I find nothing that causes me
> But sharp pain or bitter boredom.
> Nature, in her varied beauty,
> Seems to my view to wrap herself
> In sad mourning, and, her laws being broken,
> Everything precipitates itself into the antique chaos.
> Yes, my friend, yes: My soul, insensitive
> To the soft impression of vigorous pleasure,
> Darkens everything in its own sadness,
> Finding a source in everything for more grief
> And for this *fastidio universal* for which my heart
> Encounters in everything a perennial cause.[32]

There were several disciples of Meléndez who continued his outlook and innovations. None achieved his importance in the development of Spanish poetry. Among these men were Nicasio Álvarez de Cienfuegos, Manuel José Quintana, Francisco Sánchez Barbero, José Somoza, and Juan Nicasio Gallego. The first two are the most important.

Cienfuegos was born in Madrid in 1764. As a student at Salamanca he met Meléndez. He later went to Madrid, occupying a government position. It was here that his friendship with Quintana became close. He began to write drama, and in 1798 he published a volume of both plays and poems. Unlike some of his peers, he opposed the new French government in 1808 and was sent to France as a hostage. He died following his arrival there in 1809, at the age of forty-five.

His first poetry is much like the anacreontic and pastoral poetry just seen in Meléndez. Later he began to dwell more on very personal themes and to cultivate a romantic interest in solitude, death, the tomb, etc. An interest in revolution and humanitarianism is also exhibited, and with these themes he approaches more the poetic direction of Quintana. The language employed in such poems becomes more hyperbolic and exclamatory, exactly like that Quintana produces so avidly throughout the first half of the nineteenth century.

Quintana lived from 1772 to 1857, and during his rather long life he produced a great deal of poetry, most of it nationalistic in theme. When we consider the tone of the early nineteenth century, such a theme is not unexpected. In fact, precisely because of his outspoken, fervidly patriotic, and often bombastic verses Quintana should be considered the Spanish poet laureate by the time of his death. His early poetry followed the anacreontic, pastoral mode of the Salamancan School but by the beginning of the new century he had found his literary métier in the more messianic, rhetorical poetry for which he is best remembered today. More successful than Cienfuegos, Quintana was able to follow the Junta Central when the French took over the capital in 1808, and in its service he wrote exuberant proclamations and exhortations to the loyal populace. He naturally suffered on the restoration of Ferdinand VII to the throne. Not until the latter's death did he reacquire government protection. Under Isabel he reached the pinnacle of his glory not only as a poet but as a sort of defender of the national spirit. He well deserved the honors that came to him in the latter part of his life.[33]

The reader may wonder why we discuss Cadalso's *Noches lúgubres* (*Mournful Nights*) at this point, but the reason is a simple one — it is the best example of poetic prose of the period. It also, like Meléndez' poetry, signals the early advancement of Spanish romanticism. The *Mournful Nights* was written sometime between April 22, 1771, the day María Ignacia Ibáñez died, and 1774.[34] The death of this woman, the greatest actress of the day and Cadalso's mistress, inspired the work's composition. Essentially it is the story of Tediato's mourning over the death of his beloved, his attempt to disinter her body, the futility of such an act, and his realization of the value of human friendship.

It is the work's assertion of romantic tendencies, especially that of suicide, that concerns us now. In Spain it provides the antecedent of the nineteenth-century romantic custom of suicide as the final solution to one's problems. Suicide is the natural consequence of the *fastidio universal,* and it therefore in this work has as much significance as Meléndez' invention of the important romantic term. As much as announcing the lachrymose poetry of Bécquer, the theme of suicide here also recalls the despairing poetry of Garcilaso. Once more we see the continuing lines of thought and philosophy throughout the history of Spanish literature.

The *Nights* is at once a work based on literary tradition and the inventive creativeness of its composer, Cadalso. Many have seen a great influence of Young's *Night Thoughts,* but in reality this is very little. There is more from a Spanish folk tale *La difunta plei-teada (The Litigated Corpse).* The similarity of this work and Cadalso's is superficial, however, and we thus emphasize Cadalso's story because until recently his work was summarily dismissed as imitative. Its inventiveness is seen principally in its presentation of "psychological action and ambience." There is little description of surroundings and virtually no action. These essential attributes of any literary work rather take place in the mind of the hero Tediato. We intuit, much as we do in poetry, what is occurring and are strongly moved as a direct consequence of our necessary mental and emotional involvement with the mind and heart of the characters.

Before we finish our study of poetry we must mention another school that also reflected a sixteenth-century ancestor, the Sevillian School of Poetry. This was not as well known in the eighteenth century as its counterpart, yet several of its members were outstanding writers and, fortunately, are being more and more appreciated in our own day. After one or two previous ephemeral academies in Seville, a permanent Academia Particular de Letras Humanas (Private Academy of Human Letters) was founded in 1793. An undeniable impetus came from the Salamancan School, much aided by the active influence of Jovellanos and Forner. Like its predecessor of the 1500s, the School gave much attention to form and style. Neoclassic taste as a result held much greater sway here than in Salamanca as time passed.

Since the school is actually much later in its true flowering I note only three writers, very briefly. The first is José Marchena y Ruiz de Cueto or, as he is often called, the *Abate* Marchena. He was born in 1768 and died in 1821. He was an ardent politician, and during the reign of Joseph I he held several government positions. The most intriguing thing about him as a man was his personality — volatile, opinionated, honest, and aggressive in the extreme. This almost abrasive character is reflected in his work which is often outspoken. He published in different genres — plays, essays, and poetry. His verses are frequently attempts at excusing excesses of the French revolutionaries and of a revolutionary spirit in general. With such excessive politicking, his poetry is often bad as far as lyricism is concerned. Nevertheless he is certainly an excellent example of the new, more nationalistic attitudes that appear from the 1790s on, whether among poets of Salamancan or Sevillian persuasion.

José María Blanco y Crespo was born in Seville in 1775. His father was of Irish descent and later Blanco would use the original last name of White, becoming the more well-known Blanco-White. He went to England just before the French arrived in Seville. Here he eventually became involved in politics and essentially avoided his Spanish heritage until in old age he began to feel remorse for his rejection of Spain. He died in 1841 in Liverpool.

He wrote some of his works in English of which the most significant is his *Letters From Spain,* a *costumbrista* work that portrays Andalusia with amazing clarity and feeling. His poetry is very personal and revealing, often tinged with a sort of melodramatic romanticism in expression.

Alberto Lista is the most outstanding of these poets. He too was born in 1775. His personality began to define itself at the French invasion when he aligned himself with the nationalists opposed to the French occupation. The ironic thing is that he finally aligned himself with the French when they invaded Seville. It is customary to criticize him in these circumstances, but he is not unlike Meléndez, who also supported the French government.[35] Exiled for a time after the restoration of Ferdinand VII, he returned to lead an active literary life. He died in Seville in 1848.

In his own day Lista was known for his advanced ideas concerning education. The reader should see especially Hans Juretschke for more details about Lista's various interests and activities.[36] His poetry is essentially serene in tone and style; Lista was a priest, among other things. At one point we find him openly imitating the work of San Juan de la Cruz, for example. But we should not characterize his work as completely dry because the anacreontic, pastoral style of Meléndez is also found in much evidence.

V *Conclusion*

As we reach the end of this chapter we come to the conclusion of our study. We have seen that Spanish literature of the eighteenth century is quite varied in its scope, yet singular in its intent — to teach and to reform. Basically didactic, it nevertheless exhibits at all times both facets of the Horatian dictum. Such a happy combination is nowhere better seen than in Iriarte's *Literary Fables*. But this characteristic is evidenced elsewhere of course, from Feijoo and Luzán on down to such an unlikely source as Quintana. This double-faceted characteristic of the literature is extremely important, because the failure to see and understand it has been at the basis of all negative criticism of the period. In our presentation of the cultural and social directions, in our examination of the prose, the drama, and the poetry of the 1700s it is hoped that this dual aspect of the literature and the century in general is evident. If so, the reader can view the period not so much as a rigid entity unto itself but one in which lines and directions mingle and meld, at times into some of the most piercingly beautiful human expression in all Spanish literature.

Notes and References

Chapter One

1. Charles E. Chapman, *A History of Spain* (New York: Macmillan, 1918), pp. 268–71, 369–71. The reader is also referred to the following books for more detailed information on Spanish history and culture in the eighteenth century: Fernando Díaz Plaja, *La vida española en el siglo XVIII* (Barcelona: A. Martín, 1946); Richard Herr, *Spain* (Englewood Cliffs, N.J.: Prentice-Hall, 1971); Harold Livermore, *A History of Spain* (New York: Grove Press, 1960); and Vicente Palacio Atard, *Los españoles de la Ilustración* (Madrid: Ediciones Guadarrama, 1964).
2. Chapman, pp. 408–10.
3. John H. R. Polt, *Gaspar Melchor de Jovellanos* (New York: Twayne, 1971), pp. 145–46.
4. Juan Meléndez Valdes, *Biblioteca de Autores Españoles* (Madrid: Ediciones Atlas, 1952), LXIII, 200a, b.
5. Chapman, pp. 445–54.
6. Ibid., p. 461.
7. Juan Meléndez Valdés, *Discursos forenses* (Madrid: Imprenta Real, 1821), pp. 296–98, 300–301.
8. Richard Herr, *The Eighteenth-Century Revolution in Spain* (Princeton: Princeton University Press, 1958), p. 155.
9. Ibid., p. 116.
10. Chapman, pp. 465–66.
11. See my "Spain and the Founding Fathers," *The Modern Language Journal* 60 (March, 1976), 101–9.
12. Robert E. Pellissier, *The Neo-Classic Movement in Spain During the XVIII Century* (Stanford, 1918), p. 58.
13. Juan Pablo Forner, *Cotejo de las églogas que ha premiado la Real Academia de la Lengua,* ed. Fernando Lázaro (Salamanca: Consejo Superior de Investigaciones Científicas, 1951), pp. 47–48.
14. José Jurado, "Repercusiones del pleito con Iriarte en la obra de Forner," *Thesaurus* 24 (1969), 228–77.
15. Tomás de Iriarte, *Colección de obras en verso y prosa* (Madrid: En la Imprenta de Benito Cano, 1787), VI, 377–78.
16. Juan Pablo Forner, *Los gramáticos: historia chinesca,* ed. John H. R. Polt (Madrid: Editorial Castalia; Berkeley: University of California

Press, 1970); and ibid., ed, José Jurado (Madrid: Espasa-Calpe, 1970).

17. Masson de Morvilliers, "Espagne," *Encyclopédie Méthodique, Géographie* (Paris, 1783), I, 565.

Chapter Two

1. I. L. McClelland, *Benito Jerónimo Feijoo* (New York: Twayne, 1969), pp. ix–x.

2. This brief review of the polemics, authors, and books that came about as a result of Feijoo's publications is based on Juan Luis Alborg, *Historia de la literatura española. Siglo XVIII* (Madrid: Editorial Gredos, 1972), pp. 141–47. The reader is referred there for further information as well as to the selected bibliography at the end of the present volume. For information on Herculaneum one might see Wolfgang Leppman's very readable *Pompeii in Fact and Fiction* (London: Elek Books, 1968).

3. Benito Jerónimo Feijoo, *Theatro crítico universal,* 6th ed. (Madrid: Herederos de Francisco del Hierro, 1753), III, pp. 278–79. I use my own collection of Feijoo's works in quoting Feijoo. The reader is referred to McClelland's study for more complete bibliographical information.

4. Ibid., 10th ed. (Madrid: Fernández de Arrojo, 1758), I, 1, 10–11.

5. Ibid., 6th ed. (Madrid: Antonio Pérez de Soto, 1753), IV, 116–17.

6. Ibid., (Madrid: Eugenio Bicco, 1754), VII, 255.

7. Feijoo, *Cartas eruditas y curiosas,* 2d ed. (Madrid: Eugenio Bieco, 1754), IV, 353, 345–46.

8. Ibid., (Madrid: Joachim Ibarra, 1760), V, 313–14, 315.

9. See my "Cervantes and Three *Ilustrados:* Mayans, Sarmiento, and Bowle," forthcoming.

10. See my "Fray Martín Sarmiento: Personality, Style, and Poetics," *Romance Notes,* forthcoming. See Also Martín Sarmiento, *Memorias para la historia de la poesía española y poetas españoles* (Madrid: Ibarra, 1775), pp. 243–44.

11. Emilio Cotarelo y Mori, *Iriarte y su época* (Madrid: Est. Tipográfico "Sucesores de Rivadeneyra," 1897), p. 30.

12. Alborg, p. 868.

13. Gregorio Mayans y Siscar, *Vida de Miguel de Cervantes Saavedra,* ed. Antonio Mestre (Madrid: Espasa Calpe, 1972), p. 9.

14. In 1747 William Lauder published an article in the *Gentleman's Magazine* saying that Milton's *Paradise Lost* was mainly constructed of plagiaristic paraphrases of a Latin poem "Sarcotis" by Jacobus Masenius in 1654. Then in early 1750 he followed this up with a more lengthy work which aroused many scholars of the day, including John Bowle. It was entitled "An Essay on Milton's Use and Imitation of the Moderns in his *Paradise Lost.*" Lauder was a literary forger who had been highly educated (University of Edinburgh). A good classical scholar, he was disappointed in the positions he sought and as a consequence turned to lit-

erary forgery. He soon found himself in 1750 in the center of a violent scandal. No less a personage than Samuel Johnson came to his defense. Johnson's action was particularly unfortunate for himself because when Lauder was eventually revealed as a fraud Johnson too was implicated. Only his integrity and known honesty saved him from public vilification in the end. Bowle's responsibility in revealing Lauder's guilt brings him an interesting, indirect connection with Johnson. Lauder was totally humiliated. He emigrated to Barbadoes where he died in utter poverty in 1771.

15. See Eva Marja Rudat, *Las ideas estéticas de Esteban de Arteaga: Orígenes, significado y actualidad* (Madrid: Editorial Gredos, 1971).

16. Alborg, p. 920.

17. Polt, *Jovellanos,* unnumbered pages of the "Chronology."

18. Ibid., p. 76.

19. Gaspar Melchor de Jovellanos, *Obras en prosa,* ed. José Caso González (Madrid: Editorial Castalia, 1969), pp. 279–81.

20. The reader should see particularly Russell P. Sebold, *Novela y autobiografía en la "Vida" de Torres Villarroel* (Barcelona: Editorial Ariel, 1975). He should also see: the edition of the *Vida* by Federico de Onís (Madrid: Espasa-Calpe, 1954), the edition by Russell P. Sebold of Torres' *Visiones y visitas* (Madrid: Espasa-Calpe, 1966), and I. L. McClelland's *Diego de Torres Villarroel* (Boston: Twayne, 1976).

21. See Paul Ilie, "Grotesque Portraits in Torres Villarroel," *Bulletin of Hispanic Studies* 45 (1968), 16–37. See also Sebold's introduction to his edition of the *Visiones.*

22. Alborg, pp. 257–59.

23. The reader should see the excellent introduction to Sebold's edition of *Fray Gerundio* (Madrid: Espasa-Calpe, 1962).

24. Alborg, pp. 362–64.

25. Russell P. Sebold, *Colonel Don José Cadalso* (New York: Twayne, 1971), pp. 13–14.

26. José Cadalso, *Cartas marruecas* (Madrid: Espasa-Calpe, 1967), pp. 195–96.

Chapter Three

1. Alborg, p. 207.

2. For more detail on Luzán's life see: Juan Ignacio de Luzán, *Memorias de la vida de don Ignacio de Luzán,* in *BAE* (Madrid: Ediciones Atlas, 1952), LXI, 95–105; Gabriela Makowiecka, *Luzán y su poética* (Barcelona: Editorial Planeta, 1973); I. L. McClelland, *Ignacio de Luzán* (New York: Twayne, 1973).

3. Ignacio de Luzán, *La poética o Reglas de la poesía,* ed. Luigi de Filippo (Barcelona: Selecciones Bibliófilas, 1956), I, 26–28.

4. John Cook, *Neo-Classic Drama in Spain. Theory and Practice* (Dallas, 1959).

5. Alborg, p. 560.

6. Cotarelo y Mori, pp. 65–68.

7. Cook, p. 223.

8. See my *Tomás de Iriarte* (New York: Twayne, 1972), pp. 65–73.

9. Russell P. Sebold, *Colonel Don José Cadalso,* pp. 148–50.

10. Ignacio López de Ayala, *Numancia destruida,* ed. Russell P. Sebold (Salamanca: Ediciones Anaya, 1971).

11. Vicente García de la Huerta, *Raquel* (Zaragoza: Editorial Ebro, 1956), pp. 63–69.

12. Ibid., p. 71.

13. Russell P. Sebold, "Contra los mitos antineoclásicos españoles," in *El rapto de la mente* (Madrid: Editorial Prensa Española, 1970), pp. 49–56.

14. Leandro Fernández de Moratín, "Discurso preliminar," *Obras de Moratín* in *BAE* (Madrid: Imprenta de la Publicidad, 1850), II, 319.

15. Tomás de Iriarte, IV, 321, 326.

16. Iriarte, *La señorita mal criada, comedia moral en tres actos* (1788?), p. 22. (This publication is in a loose-leaf, printed form. It indicates no place of publication and the date has been penciled in.)

17. For more information on the history of the melologue the reader should see José Subirá, *El compositor Iriarte (1750–1791) y el cultivo español del melólogo (melodrama),* 2 vols. (Barcelona: Consejo Superior de Investigaciones Científicas, 1949–1950).

18. Leandro Fernández de Moratín, *La comedia nueva,* ed. John Dowling (Madrid: Editorial Castalia, 1970), pp. 18–19.

19. John H. R. Polt, "Jovellanos' *El delincuente honrado,*" *Romanic Review* 50 (1959), 170–90.

20. For more details the reader should see John A. Moore, *Ramón de la Cruz* (New York: Twayne, 1972).

21. Ramón de la Cruz, *Sainetes,* ed. José M. Castro y Calvo (Zaragoza: Editorial Ebro, 1957), pp. 35–36.

Chapter Four

1. Leopoldo Augusto de Cueto, *Bosquejo histórico-crítico de la poesía castellana en el siglo XVIII* in *BAE* (Madrid: Ediciones Atlas, 1952), LXI, xxxiii–xxxvii.

2. *Poesía del siglo XVIII,* ed. John H. R. Polt (Madrid: Editorial Castalia, 1975), p. 46.

3. Ibid., p. 48.

4. Ibid., pp. 62, 65.

5. Ibid., p. 67.

6. Ibid., p. 130.

7. Ibid., p. 133.

8. Ibid., p. 202.

9. Félix María de Samaniego, "Poesías," in *BAE,* LXI, 366.

10. Tomás de Iriarte, *Obras,* I, 1.

11. Cotarelo y Mori, p. 251.

12. François Vézinet, *Molière, Florian Et La Littérature Espagnole* (Paris: Librairie Hachette Et Cie., 1909), p. 233.

13. Ibid., p. 245.

14. Iriarte, *Literary Fables of Yriarte,* trans. George H. Devereux (Boston: Ticknor and Fields, 1855), pp. 44–45.

15. Iriarte, *Obras,* VI, 383.

16. Iriarte, trans. Devereux, p. 9.

17. Ibid., pp. 85–86.

18. Ibid., p. 34.

19. Ibid., p. 65.

20. Ibid., p. 69.

21. Ibid., p. 61.

22. Ibid., p. 122.

23. Azorín [pseud.], José Martínez Ruiz, *De Granada a Castelar* in *Obras completas* (Madrid: Aguilar, 1948), IV, 352–53.

24. Ibid., 354.

25. Ibid., 357.

26. Juan Meléndez Valdés, *BAE* (Madrid: Ediciones Atlas, 1952), LXIII, 93a.

27. Ibid., 224a.

28. Ibid., 225a.

29. Ibid., 198a.

30. Ibid., 193a.

31. Ibid., 193b.

32. Ibid., 250.

33. For further details the reader should see: Leopoldo Augusto de Cueto, *Bosquejo, BAE,* LXI, clxxviii–clxxxii; Manuel José Quintana, *Poesías completas,* ed. Albert Derozier (Madrid: Editorial Castalia, 1969); Dérozier's *Manuel Josef Quintana Et La Naissance Du Libéralisme En Espagne* (Paris, 1968); and José Vila Selma's *Ideario de Manuel José Quintana* (Madrid: Consejo Superior de Investigaciones Científicas, 1961).

34. Russell P. Sebold, *Colonel Don José Cadalso,* p. 89. For considerable detail on the *Noches lúgubres* the reader should see especially this book by Sebold and also Nigel Glendinning's "New Light on the Text and Ideas of Cadalso's *Noches lúgubres,*" *Modern Language Review* 55, 537–42, and his "The Traditional Story of 'La difunta pleiteada,' Cadalso's *Noches lúgubres,* and the Romantics," *Bulletin of Hispanic Studies* 38, 206–15. The reader may also want to consult the introduction to the *Clásicos Castellanos* edition of the *Noches,* ed. Nigel Glendinning (Madrid: Espasa-Calpe, 1961).

35. See my *Juan Meléndez Valdés* (New York: Twayne, 1974),

pp. 50–55.

36. Hans Juretschke, *Vida, obra y pensamiento de Alberto Lista* (Madrid: Consejo Superior de Investigaciones Científicas, 1951).

Selected Bibliography

ADDY, GEORGE M. *The Enlightenment in the University of Salamanca.* Durham: Duke University Press, 1966. Penetrating study of the university in the eighteenth century.

AGUILAR PIÑAL, FRANCISCO. *Bibliografía fundamental de la literatura española, siglo XVIII.* Madrid: Sociedad General Española de Librería, 1976. Valuable reference work.

———. *Los comienzos de la crisis universitaria en España (Antología de textos del siglo XVIII).* Madrid: Editorial Magisterio, 1967. A general work on the theme of higher education.

ALBORG, JUAN LUIS. *Historia de la literatura española, siglo XVIII,* III. 3 vols. Madrid: Editorial Gredos, 1972. A new history of Spanish literature of this period containing some good insights.

ALTAMIRA Y CREVEA, RAFAEL. *Historia de España y de la civilización española.* 4 vols. Barcelona: J. Gili, 1900–1914. Study of Spanish history with penetrating ideas on the eighteenth century.

———. *Manual de historia de España.* Buenos Aires, 1946. A shorter but more accessible history by Altamira.

ANDIOC, RENÉ. *Sur La Querelle Du Théâtre Au Temps De Leandro Fernández de Moratín.* Tarbes, 1970. Important study of Spanish theater in the second half of the eighteenth century.

ARMESTO, VICTORIA. *Dos gallegos: Feijoo y Sarmiento.* La Coruña: Imprenta Moret, 1964. Brief, cogent discussion of these two scholars.

CASO GONZÁLEZ, JOSÉ et al. *Los conceptos de rococó, neoclasicismo y prerromanticismo en la literatura española del siglo XVIII.* Oviedo: Cátedra Feijoo, 1970. Good analysis of the different artistic concepts in Spanish literature of the 1700s.

CASO GONZÁLEZ, JOSÉ. *La poética de Jovellanos.* Madrid: Editorial Prensa Española, 1972. Excellent investigation of Jovellanos' poetic works.

CHAPMAN, CHARLES E. *A History of Spain.* New York: Macmillan, 1918. Good study in English of Spanish history.

CIPLIJAUSKAITÉ, BIRUTÉ. "Lo nacional en el siglo XVIII español." *Archivum* 22 (1972), 99–122. A precise presentation of the nationalistic attitude evidenced in eighteenth-century Spanish works.

COBBAN, ALFRED, ed. *The Eighteenth Century: Europe in the Age of Enlightenment.* New York: McGraw-Hill, 1969. Excellent portrayal of the arts and sciences of the 1700s. Beautiful photographs.

151

COLFORD, WILLIAM E. *Juan Meléndez Valdés*. New York: Hispanic Institute, 1942. An early, very detailed study of Meléndez.

COOK, JOHN A. *Neo-Classic Drama in Spain. Theory and Practice.* Dallas: Southern Methodist University Press, 1959. Excellent study of the neoclassic theater in Spain.

COTARELO Y MORI, EMILIO. *Don Ramón de la Cruz y sus obras.* Madrid: 1899. An early, fair investigation of this significant dramatist.

_____. *Iriarte y su época.* Madrid: Est. Tipográfico "Sucesores de Rivadeneyra," 1897. One of the most important studies on Iriarte and the eighteenth century in Spain. A monumental work.

COUGHLIN, E. V. *Antología de la poesía española del siglo XVIII.* Mexico City: Representaciones y Servicios de Ingeniería, 1971. A short collection of representative poets of the period.

COX, R. MERRITT. *An English Ilustrado: The Reverend John Bowle.* Bern: Peter Lang et Cie., 1977. A biography of this important eighteenth-century English Hispanist.

_____. *Juan Meléndez Valdés.* New York: Twayne, 1974. A general study of Meléndez, with emphasis on his advancement of romanticism in Spain.

_____. *The Rev. John Bowle: The Genesis of Cervantean Criticism.* Chapel Hill: University of North Carolina Press, 1971. An investigation of Bowle's 1781 edition of *Don Quixote* and its impact on modern Cervantean criticism.

_____. *Tomás de Iriarte.* New York: Twayne, 1972. A general study of Iriarte.

CUETO, LEOPOLDO AUGUSTO DE. *Poetas líricos del siglo XVIII.* 3 vols. In *BAE,* vols. 61, 63, 67. (Madrid: Ediciones Atlas, 1952–1953). Easily accessible collection of poetry of the Spanish eighteenth century.

DEMERSON, GEORGES. *Don Juan Meléndez Valdés Et Son Temps (1754–1817).* Paris: Librairie C. Klincksieck, 1962. There is a Spanish translation: *Don Juan Meléndez Valdés y su tiempo (1754–1817),* 2 vols. (Madrid: Taurus Ediciones, 1971). The most authoritative and exhaustive study of Meléndez available.

DEMERSON, JORGE, DEMERSON, PAULA DE, and AGUILAR PIÑAL, FRANCISCO. *Las Sociedades Económicas de Amigos del País en el siglo XVIII.* San Sebastián: Gráficas Izarra, 1974. Authoritative study of the economic societies.

DÉROZIER, ALBERT. *Manuel Josef Quintana Et La Naissance Du Libéralisme En Espagne.* Paris, 1968. An essential work for the comprehension of this enigmatic poet and his relation to his times.

DÍAZ PLAJA, FERNANDO. *La vida española en el siglo XVIII.* Barcelona: A. Martín, 1946. Good cultural survey of the period.

DOWLING, JOHN. "*Capricho* as Style in Life, Literature, and Art from Zamora to Goya." *Eighteenth-Century Studies* 10 (Summer, 1977), 413–33. *Capricho* as an aesthetic element in the 1700s.

_____. *Leandro Fernández de Moratín.* New York: Twayne, 1971. A general study of Moratín.

_____. *"Moratín's Circle of Friends: Intellectual Ferment in Spain, 1780–1800."* *Studies in Eighteenth-Century Culture* 5 (1976), 165–83. A concise analysis of Moratín's friends.

FORNER, JUAN PABLO. *Los gramáticos: Historia chinesca.* Edited by John H. R. Polt. Madrid: Editorial Castalia; Berkeley: University of California Press, 1970. Polt's presentation of Forner is quite fair in its judgments. Excellent documentation.

_____. *Los gramáticos: Historia chinesca.* Edited by José Jurado. Madrid: Espasa-Calpe, 1970. It is curious that two editions of this previously unedited work should appear in the same year. From the standpoint of sound scholarship and accurate documentation, Polt's edition is to be preferred.

GALINO CARRILLO, M. A. *Tres hombres y un problema. Feijoo, Sarmiento y Jovellanos ante la educación moderna.* Madrid: Consejo Superior de Investigaciones Científicas, 1953. Valuable information on ideas concerning education in the 1700s.

GAY, PETER. *The Enlightenment: An Interpretation.* London: Weindenfeld and Nicholson, 1966–1970. 2 vols. Excellent interpretation of the European eighteenth century by an important scholar.

GLENDINNING, NIGEL. *A Literary History of Spain. The Eighteenth Century.* London: Ernest Benn; New York: Barnes and Noble, 1972. A general study of the Spanish eighteenth century.

_____. *"The Traditional Story of 'La difunta pleiteada': Cadalso's 'Noches lúgubres' and the Romantics."* *Bulletin of Hispanic Studies* 38 (1961), 206–15. Important investigation of an early Spanish work and its relation to Cadalso's romantic opus.

GLOVER, MICHAEL. *Legacy of Glory.* New York: Scribners', 1971. An investigation that provides sound, new ideas about the Bonaparte rule in Spain from 1808 to 1813.

GODOY, MANUEL. *Memorias.* In *BAE,* vols. 88–89. Madrid: Ediciones Atlas, 1956. Interesting for its personal tone from a man who was in the midst of the national difficulties in Spain from about 1790 to 1808.

HAMILTON, MARY NEAL. *Music in Eighteenth-Century Spain.* Illinois Studies in Language and Literature, no. 22. Urbana: University of Illinois Press, 1937. A good companion to Subirá's study although it is more general in presentation.

HARGREAVES-MAWDSLEY, W. N. *Spain Under the Bourbons, 1700–1833.* Columbia: University of South Carolina Press, 1973. Fascinating book containing a detailed introduction to the period and selected quotations from documents which illustrate the Spanish eighteenth century very well.

HATZFELD, HELMUT. *The Rococo: Eroticism, Wit and Elegance in Euro-*

pean Literature. New York: Pegasus, 1972. Definitive study of this artistic movement.

HELMAN, EDITH. *Trasmundo de Goya*. Madrid: Revista de Occidente, 1963. Basic work for the comprehension of Goya.

HERR, RICHARD. *Spain*. Englewood Cliffs, N.J.: Prentice-Hall, 1971. A series of essaylike chapters in which eighteenth-century Spain is treated with understanding.

_____. *The Eighteenth-Century Revolution in Spain*. Princeton: Princeton University Press, 1969. Contains several important insights concerning what this century really is in Spain.

HERRERO, JAVIER. *Los orígenes del pensamiento reaccionario español*. Madrid: Edicusa, 1971. Valuable study of political and cultural thought, with much pertinence to the eighteenth century.

ILIE, PAUL. "Grotesque Portraits in Torres Villarroel." *Bulletin of Hispanic Studies* 44 (1968), 16–37. Significant investigation of Torres' style.

_____. "Franklin and Villarroel: Social Consciousness in Two Autobiographies." *Eighteenth-Century Studies* 7 (1974), 321–42. Interesting comparison of these two intriguing figures of the 1700s.

IRIARTE, TOMÁS DE. *Literary Fables of Yriarte*. Translated by George H. Devereux. Boston: Ticknor and Fields, 1855. Good English translation of interest as an example of American investigations concerning Iriarte.

KANY, C. E. *Life and Manners in Madrid, 1750–1800*. Berkeley: University of California Press, 1932; reprint ed., New York: AMS Press, 1970. An important cultural presentation of the period.

JOVELLANOS, GASPAR MELCHOR DE. *Obras en prosa*. Edited by José Caso González. Madrid: Editorial Castalia, 1969. A readily available selection of Jovellanos' works in prose.

JURADO, JOSÉ. "Repercusiones del pleito con Iriarte en la obra literaria de Forner." *Thesaurus* 24 (1969), 228–77. Too long, but a good article on the facts of the polemic between Forner and Iriarte that began in 1781.

JURETSCHKE, HANS. *España ante Francia*. Madrid: Editorial Nacional, 1940. A study of Spanish-French relations from 1700 to 1850.

_____. *Los afrancesados en la guerra de independencia: Su génesis, desarrollo y consecuencias históricas*. Madrid: Ediciones Rialp, 1962. Provides new light on the Bonaparte period. A good companion to Glover's work.

_____. *Vida, obra y pensamiento de Alberto Lista*. Madrid: Consejo Superior de Investigaciones Científicas, 1951. Detailed account of Lista and his times.

LAUGHRIN, M. F. *Juan Pablo Forner as a Critic*. Washington: Catholic University of America Press, 1943. An adequate analysis of this acerbic critic.

LIVERMORE, HAROLD. *A History of Spain.* New York: Grove Press, 1960. Contains a chapter on the eighteenth century that presents many cogent facts.

LLORENTE, JUAN ANTONIO. *The History of the Inquisition of Spain from the Time of Its Establishment to the Reign of Ferdinand VII.* London: Geo. B. Whittaker, 1826. A fascinating history of this Spanish institution with many salient points about various sixteenth-, seventeenth-, and eighteenth-century figures.

LÓPEZ, FRANÇOIS. "La historia de las ideas en el siglo XVIII: concepciones antiguas y revisiones necesarias." In *Boleín del Centro de estudios del Siglo XVIII (BOCES, XVIII),* vol. 3, Oviedo: Universidad de Oviedo, 1975. pp. 3–18. A concise revelation of changing philosophical attitudes in the 1700s in Spain.

LUZÁN, IGNACIO DE. *La poética o reglas de la poesía.* Edited by Luigi de Filippo. 2 vols. Barcelona: Selecciones Bibliófilas, 1956. A limited, twentieth-century edition of Luzán's work.

LUZÁN, JUAN IGNACIO DE. *Memorias de la vida de don Ignacio de Luzán.* In *BAE,* vol. 61, pp. 95–105. Madrid: Ediciones Atlas, 1952. An easily obtained and intimate study by Luzán's son.

MAKOWIECKA, GABRIELA. *Luzán y su poética.* Barcelona: Editorial Planeta, 1973. Good analysis of Luzán and his work.

MAYANS Y SISCAR, GREGORIO. *Vida de Miguel de Cervantes Saavedra.* Edited by Antonio Mestre. Madrid: Espasa Calpe, 1972. Excellent introduction to this important Cervantean scholar.

MCCLELLAND, I. L. *Benito Jerónimo Feijoo.* New York: Twayne, 1969. A general study of Feijoo.

———. *Ignacio de Luzán.* New York: Twayne, 1973. A general study of Luzán.

———. *Spanish Drama of Pathos: 1750-1808.* 2 vols. Toronto: University of Toronto Press, 1970. Valuable study of Spanish eighteenth-century drama.

———. *The Origins of the Romantic Movement in Spain.* Liverpool: Institute of Hispanic Studies, 1937; reprint ed., Barnes and Noble, 1975. An early study of the beginnings of the romantic movement in Spain, that is, the eighteenth century.

MENÉNDEZ Y PELAYO, MARCELINO. *Historia de los heterodoxos españoles.* Edited by Enrique Sánchez Reyes. 8 vols. Santander: Aldus, 1947. Volumes 35–42 of the Edición Nacional de las Obras Completas de Menéndez Pelayo. A monumental study of important figures in Spanish history and literature, often prejudicial to those of the eighteenth century.

———. *Historia de las ideas estéticas en España.* Edited by Enrique Sánchez Reyes. 5 vols. Santander: Aldus, 1940. Volumes 1–5 of the Edición Nacional de las Obras Completas de Menéndez Pelayo. Valuable recounting of philosophical and artistic currents.

MERCADIER, GUY. *Diego de Torres Villarroel: Masques Et Miroirs.* 3 vols. Lille: Université de Lille, 1976. Exhaustive new study of the personality and work of Torres.

MOORE, JOHN. *Ramón de la Cruz.* New York: Twayne, 1972. A general study of Ramón de la Cruz.

PALACIO ATARD, VICENTE. *Los españoles de la Ilustración.* Madrid: Ediciones Guadarrama, 1964. Very good for study of culture in the eighteenth century in Spain.

PELLISSIER, ROBERT E. *The Neo-Classic Movement in Spain During the XVII Century.* Leland Stanford Junior University Publications University Series, no. 30. Stanford: Stanford University Press, 1918. A well-written, brief study that is a good companion to Cook's investigations.

PENSADO, J. L. *Fray Martín Sarmiento: sus ideas lingüísticas.* Oviedo: Cuadernos de la Cátedra Feijoo, 1960.

PETRIE, SIR CHARLES. *King Charles III of Spain: An enlightened Despot.* London: Constable, 1971. Very readable biography.

POLT, JOHN H. R. *Gaspar Melchor de Jovellanos.* New York: Twayne, 1971. A general study of Jovellanos.

_____, ed. *Poesía del siglo XVIII.* Madrid: Editorial Castalia, 1975. Excellent, readily available, and rather complete anthology of eighteenth-century Spanish poetry.

RUBIO, ANTONIO. *La crítica del galicismo en España (1726-1832).* Mexico City: La Universidad Nacional de México, 1937. An excellent synoptic view of the pro- and anti-French sentiments of major writers of this period.

RUDAT, E. M. *Las ideas estéticas de Esteban de Arteaga: Orígenes, significado y actualidad.* Madrid: Editorial Gredos, 1971. Detailed analysis of Arteaga, his work, and the advancement of eighteenth-century aesthetics.

SARRAILH, JEAN. *L'Espagne Éclairée De La Seconde Moitié Du XVIII Siècle.* Paris: Imprimerie Nationale, 1954. Good cultural, sociological, political study of the period.

SEBOLD, RUSSELL P. *Colonel Don José Cadalso.* New York: Twayne, 1971. A general study of Cadalso.

_____. *El rapto de la mente: poética y poesía dieciochescas.* Madrid: Editorial Prensa Española, 1970. Excellent series of articles on various literary subjects of the Spanish eighteenth century.

_____. "Enlightenment Philosophy and the Emergence of Spanish Romanticism." In *The Ibero-American Enlightenment,* edited by A. Owen Aldridge, pp. 111–40. Urbana: University of Illinois Press, 1971. Valuable analysis of the origins and early development of romanticism in Spain.

_____. *Novela y autobiografía en la "Vida" de Torres Villarroel.* Barcelona: Editorial Ariel, 1975. Significant new study of Torres' novelistic technique.

SEMPERE Y GUARINOS, JUAN. *Ensayo de una biblioteca de los mejores escritores del reynado de Carlos III.* 6 vols. Madrid: Imprenta Real, 1785-1789. Brief accounts of these writers and their works. Outstanding as a contemporary commentary. There is a facsimile reprint of this work made in 1963 in three volumes by the Dolphin Book Company.

SMITH, GILBERT. *Juan Pablo Forner.* Boston: Twayne, 1976. A general study of Forner.

SUBIRÁ, JOSÉ. *El compositor Iriarte (1750-1791) y el cultivo del melólogo) (melodrama).* 2 vols. Barcelona: Consejo Superior de Investigaciones Científicas, 1949-1950. Fascinating investigation of a little known genre; contains résumés de melólogos.

VÉZINET, FRANÇOIS. *Moliére, Florian Et La Littérature Espagnole.* Paris: Librairie Hachette Et Cie., 1909. A small but interesting volume of mutual influences of certain French and Spanish writers.

Index

DATE DUE			
GAYLORD			PRINTED IN U.S.A.